Dalitekklesia:

A Church from Below

Reimagining Church as Event: Perspectives from the Margins
Series Editors: George Zachariah and Sudipta Singh

In these eleven volumes, a collective of Indian theologians envisions Church as an Event that happens in particular contexts in the life of the communities at the margins. They argue that in the life of the communities who experience on their bodies the violence and hegemony of dominant power relations, morality, and religious dogmas and practices, the church happens as countercultural experiences that disrupt the logic of the prevailing order. These experiences enable and empower them to affirm and celebrate their differences, knowledges and beauty even as they weave their liberation. Church as event is a call to rising to life, creating life-flourishing communities that live out the foretaste of the reign of God.

Titles in this Series

Church and Religious Diversity Joshua Samuel and Samuel Mall
Church and Gender Justice Aruna Gnanadason
Faith in the Age of Empire Y.T. Vinayaraj
Dalitekklesia: A Church from Below Raj Bharat Patta
Church and Climate Justice Vinod Wesley
Church and Disability Samuel George
Church and Diakonia in the Age of COVID-19 Mothy Varkey
Decolonising Oikoumene Gladson Jathanna
Church and Human Sexuality Arvind Theodore
With Many Voices: Liturgies in Context Viji Varghese Eapen (Ed.)
The Word becoming Flesh George Zachariah

Dalitekklesia: A Church from Below

Raj Bharat Patta

2020

This book is dedicated to my dear grandparents,

Patta Rajaratnam & Patta Annamma,

Palaparthi Deva Raju & Palaparthi Lakshmikanthamma,

for their commitment to the Christian gospel,

for their dedication to the Church,

for their proud Dalit Christian legacy, and

for inspiring us to be a Church that brings difference in the lives of our community

Contents

Part I:
The Locality of *Dalitekklesia: Peta*

Part II:
The Locus of *Dalitekklesia*: Perspectives

Part III:
The Location of *Dalitekklesia*: Public Witness

Foreword

Discernment and radical engagement (Dare) is an initiative of the Council for World Mission (CWM) to enable faith communities to *clarify what it means to engage in* public witness to God's justice and peace in a corrupt and conflicted world.

> The mission of Dare is conceived as the coming together of (a) the *radical soul* of discernment and sense-making in theology and biblical criticism; (b) the yearnings for *signifying engagement* that rise out of the slums of modernism and the valleys of despair; and (c) the commitment to redemption songs that *inspire disturbance* at the hubs of power.

As part of the DARE initiative, each region of CWM is invited to prepare and share biblical and theological resources on current themes and issues being considered by CWM, drawing upon the experiences and resources from the region.

Interfaith Engagement, Ecumenism and Inclusive communities against dehumanising social categorisations are the themes for the book series undertaken by the South Asia region of CWM. The thrust is centred on **Reimagining Church as Event: Perspectives from the Margins**. It calls to the fore persons living in the margins and highlights their voice, their narratives and their passion for a rearrangement of life in communities, as we know it, and a commitment to rise to life and to break out from Babylon. These books are intended for the use of lay people, pastors and evangelists as well as for theological students and seminaries. The series offer stories and narratives, analyses, liturgical resources, biblical, theological and ethical reflections, and missional/praxis proposals.

Church is an event that happens at the margins of contemporary life. Church happens as an epiphanic event where the divine presence is manifested and experienced in the pathos, struggles, contestations and harmonies of everyday existence. Church happens in those spaces where we celebrate the presence of Jesus, the Christ, in the flourishing of life. Church happens when we are transformed by one another, and inspired and enabled to engage in the transformative politics of the reign of God. Church happens whenever and wherever spirit-filled communities reclaim their subversive moral agency and contest the logic and practices of domination and exclusion. Church happens when the community experiences the healing power of the wounded healer and join Jesus in this risk-taking mission, despite the wounds we bear. To reimagine Church requires courage and commitment to engage in the mission of nurturing and organising communities of resistance and healing. This book series is a humble attempt at exposing and encouraging this radical expression of Church.

I appreciate and thank all those who are associated with this series, the authors, the contributors, the publishers and the editors. I commend this book series in the hope and prayers that they will help the faith communities in South Asia, and beyond, to *discern God's presence in community and dare to engage* in ways that re-present the God of life in communities and in the public square, *Rising to Life: Living out the New Heaven and New Earth.*

Colin Cowan
General Secretary
Council for World Mission

Introduction
*Praveen P.S. Perumalla**

Indian Christian theology moves beyond the confines of dominant religious resources to become inclusive through *Dalitekklesia*. *Dalitekklesia* is a movement of Dalit Christians, accompanied by Christian theologians, which is evolving and embracing Dalit heterogeneity. Not that the way forward is without hurdles, for it chooses to swim against the odds posed by the orthodoxy of missionary theology and the dominant claims by a stream of Indian Christian theology. For these theological approaches, there are no Dalit resources as such for theological knitting, except for Dalit subservience. This, subsequently, deprives Dalit Christians of readily available theological history for reference to build upon; it is something privileged by missionary and Indian Christian theologies. Therefore, Dalit Christians are compelled to hew their own cisterns; construct theology out of the language of their workplace, from their histories of caste enslavement, from symbols of negation, and tell the stories of God's revelation; strive relentlessly to fathom the politics that create smokescreens to cover Dalit struggles and Dalit collectiveness. They could engage in the construction of biblical and theological reflections from Dalit resources, a narrow, yet, sure way forward.

The *theological* about *Dalitekklesia* starts with the *non-theological*, listening to the sciences of society that have developed empirical, observational, participatory and case-study approaches, which are relevant to Dalit studies. Yet, they are susceptible to distortions. The sciences of society are deployed to distort Dalit heterogeneity and turn sciences into ideologies. There are 59 Dalit sub-castes recognised by the state of Andhra Pradesh, of which two form the majority of Dalit communities in terms of population. Indian caste (party) politics recognise only the major Dalit communities as representatives of the rest. As a result, selective inclusion takes place, excluding the rest. The ramifications of this are Dalit segregation, weakening of Dalit solidarity and deepening of Dalit dependency on caste people. Segregated Dalit communities are indoctrinated by an antagonistic ideology, resulting in viewing fellow Dalits as potential enemies. But, the very design of Indian democracy is to overcome caste (party) politics through democratisation of the Indian economy, politics and social life. Dr. B.R. Ambedkar's approach is to democratise the economic, social and political life of a nation through constitutional provisions. This includes budgetary obligations to allot a designated percentage of the total budget for the welfare of Dalits and Adivasis.

The sciences of society hardly paid attention to such democratisation of the national economy until the diversion of funds scam was unearthed by Dalit movements. An exploration of the intricacies of democracy reveals just how much it is binding on the state as well as the Central government's budgetary planning to empower Dalits and Adivasis—a case for the Scheduled Castes and Scheduled Tribes Sub-Plan. It is the failure on the part of civil society in advancing democratic politics that cost the democratisation of different ministries to prevail upon caste politics. This made it possible for the diversion of allocated resources for Dalits and Adivasis and, further, the abolition of the Planning Commission. With the slowing down of democratic politics, caste politics has thrived upon perpetuating antagonism within the Dalit communities, between Dalits and Adivasis, and Dalits and Other Backward Classes. The social and cultural identities, which were to elucidate the prevailing web of social relations, have been changed to accommodate the agenda of hate and antagonism, by which it impairs sociocultural solidarity in civil society.

In view of the above analysis of democracy and caste, *Dalitekklesia,* which is a theological and civil society component, is immune neither to the universe of sciences of society nor to caste politics. An uncritical incorporation of the said distortions and diversions constrains democracy and the building of a vibrant civil society. For *Dalitekklesia,* it is not enough to be conscious about various constraints; as it elucidates Dalit heterogeneity in theological language, it needs to nurture Dalit solidarity prophetically while addressing the ideologies and politics of antagonism, broaden democratic spaces, and create spaces for Dalit and Adivasi communities and Dalit Bahujan solidarity.

Dalitekklesia is grounded on Dalit pathos that manifests with the negation of human rights and legal remedies. First, Dalit Christians are barred from the communal award that privileges them for economic, political and legal safeguards; second, there is an indifferent attitude among Dalit and Christian parliamentarians; third, the alienation among fellow Dalits weakens Dalit solidarity and gives space for contemptuous feelings; fourth, the orthodoxy of missionary theology and Indian Christian theology lacks adequate scope for conversation with Dalits, with religions opted by Dalits, namely Buddhism and Islam, with Dalit social movements lead by Iyothee Thass, Bhagya Reddy Varma, Jotirao Phule, Dr. B.R. Ambedkar and others, and with movements for democracy; fifth, there is a lack of conscious effort to train and promote Dalit Christian leadership in the church, in bureaucracy and politics to widen democratic spaces; and sixth, Dalit women and culture for social transformation are subsumed under caste structures and practices.

It is based on the above postulates that I read *Dalitekklesia*, a good work by my friend Raj Bharat Patta, a Dalit Christian theologian and Pastor, well introduced through his work with the ecumenical circles in India and elsewhere. He has put forth field knowledge acquired while he worked with the National Council of Churches in India and as a Pastor for Dalit Christian churches in the Telugu region. His desire to broaden the scope of *Dalitekklesia* to be dialogical by engaging with the works of Dr. B.R. Ambedkar for a theological praxis finds relevance in building Dalit solidarity and theology. His imaginative conversation engaging three prominent progressive contexts—his own Dalit Christian identity, the Martin Luther Reformation tradition, and the Ecumenical initiatives by the Pope—is very interesting, opening a new window to the history of Christianity from *Dalitekklesia*. I wish that *Dalitekklesia* engages the Indian church in serious discussions on the framework of democracy and caste. I congratulate him for his promising work, and also the Council for World Mission for publishing it, especially the initiatives taken by Dr. Sudipta Singh. I do place on record a word of gratitude to Dr. George Zachariah, my companion and colleague in my formation and vocation as theological educator, for inviting me to write an introduction to this book.

* **The Rev. Dr. Praveen P.S. Perumalla** serves the Church of South India Synod as Liaison Officer for the Evangelical Mission in Solidarity, Germany. He is an ordained minister of the Church of South India, Diocese of Karimnagar. He served the Andhra Christian Theological College, Hyderabad, as Professor in the Department of Social Analysis (Theology), and taught at the Gurukul Lutheran Theological College and Research Institute, Chennai, and the University of Madras, Department of Christian Studies.

Acknowledgements

This book, *Dalitekklesia: A Church from Below*, has only been possible because of the generosity of the Council for World Mission (CWM), and especially because of my two dear and respectable friends, the editors of this series, Sudipta Singh and George Zachariah. Many thanks to CWM and to Sudipta *Dada* and George *Anna*. Thank you for taking my ideas on board of this series and for your constant encouragement.

I have dedicated this book to my dear grandparents, who deserve to be acknowledged here for the positive influence they have had on me and on my family in celebrating our proud Dalit Christian roots and for their rich Dalit Christian legacy. They aren't here to receive this book, but this book is a tribute to all their contributions to the church from below.

I also need to place on record my gratitude to my dear parents, Patta Deva Raju and Patta Indira, for all their love and support throughout my life. They have truly lived up to their Dalit Christian calling and contributed untiringly and passionately towards the transformation of the church and society. Both my dad and mom will always be my heroes, for they made me understand and helped me to reflect about the church from below, right from our daily family prayers.

I thank Bethany Peta, our Dalit Christian locality for all the nurture I have received there. I thank the Andhra Evangelical Lutheran Church, the Gurukul Lutheran Theological College, the National Council of Churches in India, the Student Christian Movement of India and the wider ecumenical movement for challenging me to explore *Dalitekklesia*, theologically and missionally at various settings, and for providing me opportunities to contribute most of the writings in this book about a church from below. I also thank The University of Manchester, the Methodist Church in the United Kingdom, my circuit here, and several other theological and ecumenical agencies in the UK for their support to my Dalit theological endeavours.

My dear wife Shiny and our two wonderful sons Jubi and Jaiho have always stood by me with love and care all through my journey. They coped with my extended hours in my reading room and have always supported my passion for a church from below. Any words of gratitude are insufficient to them; however, I thank them for all their unconditional love and support. I also thank all our family members, cousins and friends who encouraged me and my writings.

I thank God, the broken, crucified and risen Jesus Christ, who continually inspires and challenges me towards a church from below, offering to be a collaborator and a companion in striving for *Dalitekklesia*.

Prologue

As this book goes for publication, the church has moved online in many places in the world due to the COVID-19 lockdown. Social distancing has been a catchword to keep safe during this pandemic. One of the posters that I saw outside a church building was, "This building is closed, but church is open." The understanding of the church as a building has changed, because church as people has become more open and meaningful through the acts of kindness in communities today. Many people in various contexts have been engaging in discussing the meaning and relevance of the church during this lockdown. *Dalitekklesia: A Church from Below* is an offering to the global reimagining of church today, offering perspectives and possibilities of being and becoming a church relevant for our times.

Dalits, even prior to this lockdown, have always been kept at a social distance because of the notion of purity and pollution, a key ideological pillar of the caste system, just because they were born outside of the caste hierarchy. Experiencing social distancing is nothing new to us as Dalits. However, it was the gospel of Jesus that paved the way for reducing that gap. With the arrival of the Christian gospel, my grandfather and his generation became Christians and have been part of the Christian church for about four generations now. As Dalit Christians, we have become a Dalit church in our locality. We have been a Dalit church, which I call *Dalitekklesia: A Church From Below*, that is evolving out of our own Dalit Christian ethos and values.

In the Gospel according to St. Mark 7:31-37, we find Jesus healing a person who is differently abled, suffering from hearing and speech problems. The significant part of this healing is the role of a community, or a group of people, in the healing of this person. If we carefully read through this passage, we see that the healing takes place in an **unknown place** (no clear place is mentioned), the healing happens to an **unknown person** (no name or identity of the person is mentioned), the people who bring the sick person to Jesus is an **unknown community** (it is only mentioned 'they', with no other clue of who they are), and Jesus uses an **unusual way of healing** (taking aside the person to a private place, putting his fingers in his ears, touching his tongue with his saliva, looking up to heaven, sighing and saying "Ephphatha") to transform the person to a known one 'as his own one.'

The emphasis in this episode is on the role of the **unknown community**, which played a vital role in the healing process. I strongly feel the relevance of this community, which when I read through my Dalit theological lens I recognise as *Dalitekklesia*. They were a church from below. This **unknown community**, which I would like to call as *Dalitekklesia*, was instrumental in making the unknown place a known one, for it would remain as a historic place for healing. This community transformed the person, his life and his future. I wonder whether Jesus healed the person, marveling at the faith of this community. The community's faith would have made news headlines in their days; and had the writer of Hebrews known about this community, he/she would have added this community to the list of heroes and sheroes of faith mentioned in chapter 11. This community was a group of unsung heroes and sheroes, who did not crave for their names to be a banner, but rather concentrated on their neighbour and his healing.

Dalitekklesia: A church from below is a church that seeks and facilitates healing for their neighbours. These six characters explains their DNA.

- It was an unknown community—for no identity is mentioned.

- It was a voicing community—for it became the voice for this voiceless person.

- It was a faith community—but for their faith, the person would not have been healed.

- It was an open community—with no barriers, for even the sick and weak were its members.

- It was a proclaiming community—it zealously proclaimed the healer and the healing.

- It was a loving community—it showed concern for the neighbour.

What is the locus, where is the locality and where is the location of the church today in India? These are the questions that this book, *Dalitekklesia: A Church From Below*, primarily engages with. The margins in India are nothing new, as most of the church and society are defined in terms of purity and pollution, privilege and prestige, or principalities and powers, leaving a major chunk of people and perspectives as powerless and on the margins. This book's locus is on understanding God, church and theology from the perspectives of Dalits, who have been pushed to the margins for ages as they have been outcast(e)s in the hierarchical caste system. In a way, *Dalitekklesia*: A Church From Below, offers a Dalit understanding of God as a suffering God, and offers the church as a church of the margins, recognising and acknowledging the agency of Dalits in this endeavour. The locality of the Indian church is discussed by bringing in the contextual social analysis of the margins, particularly discussing the locality as *Peta*, which is used for Dalit localities. The location of the church is defined by its public witness and therefore this book offers some perspectives in that direction of reimagining the church from below.

The aim of this book is to engage in critical reflection on the very understanding of church from below, for the church traditionally has been understood as a hierarchical church running on the model of exercising power top-down. This book is an invitation for all those people who see the vision of a church bottom-up, where powers and principalities are dismantled. When all our churches are and become churches from below, the vision towards a new creation is possible.

This book, *Dalitekklesia: A Church from Below*, is a compilation of several reflections over a period of time. Each of these were written at a given point of time, and I had to revisit them and edit them so that they fit into the flow of discussions here. As readers you will notice that editing and also recognise that each article was written in a particular time and context. Some of these reflections were published in other journals and books as stand-alone articles. Most of them are also found on my personal blog, *thepattas.blogspot.com*. I have never dreamt that all these articles would one day become part of a book. Thanks to the Council for World Mission, particularly to Sudipta Singh, who I always acknowledge as the one dipping me "into the baptism of fire in ecumenism," and to George Zachariah, my friend and mentor who supported my theological engagements right from the beginning of my career, for inviting me to this book project. I was nostalgic as I was bringing these articles together, for I remembered the context in which each of these evolved, and am thankful to all those who challenged and inspired me to keep writing.

As we all know, the word *Ekklesia* originally referred to the political assembly in the Athenian democratic system in the early Greek period, where male citizens who had done two years of work in the army were summoned and gathered to debate and discuss the various political issues of their day. Eventually the word came to be associated with the church, and the power structures continued to exist across histories and geographies. *Dalitekklesia,* as a church from below, deconstructs such notions of power ascribed to the church, and affirms a just and inclusive community where all are invited to gather and celebrate the love of God. Here, I should also mention that this book is not one discussing the doctrine of the church, but it is a rainbow of reflections on the church from Dalit perspectives.

Reimagining the Birthing of a New Church Today

If Pentecost served as a birthing experience for the early church, which was primarily based on the rediscovery of inclusion, margins and resistance, during this lockdown, in 2020, how do we reimagine the birthing of a new church? Perhaps the rediscovery of the early church might serve as a signpost in our reimagining of the church today, and *Dalitekklesia* is an offering to such a conversation. These are the questions that this offering discusses in the chapters to follow.

1. As a church that needs to take a rebirth today, the question that is still relevant is who is in and who is out. Who decides the boundaries? Can the boundaries be burnt by the fire of the Spirit, so that all—all means all—are included?

2. Are we as a church able to be understood by those people on the margins today? Are we speaking in languages that people in our communities are able to hear and understand? As a church, how do we recognise the role and functions of excluded communities today?

3. Are we as a church subsumed by the language of the powerful or are we joining with the divine Spirit, by resisting to speak the language of power, to seek to identify with those people on the margins by speaking their language?

The Spirit of Pentecost invites us to dream, to reimagine and to envision the birthing of a church that is relevant, open, resisting powers and being with and among the people on the margins. This book, *Dalitekklesia,* grapples with the above-mentioned questions and invites the readers to participate in reimagining a church relevant for the times. In that reimagination, I have two dreams for my *Dalitekklesia* as it journeys forward.

First, my dream is for an *Ubuntu* church where we find the meaning of our existence only in relation to our community. An "I am because we are" kind of church. The longing of the community becomes our priority, the language that the public sphere understands today will be our communication, and the location of the margins becomes our dwelling and serving place. Second, my dream is for a 'Fluid church' that is not bound by principalities and powers, but which takes its course following Jesus, the living water, in watering people's lives and striving to quench the thirst of creation. This kind of a church can be online, offline, inline and out of line, but a church that is willing to flow into the corners of a village, into our *Petas* and into the highways of the city, meeting people where they are and working with them for food, peace and justice. In order to achieve our dreams, we need to be open to the Spirit of God so that we are led by her and give up all that is me, mine and myself and take on we, us and together so that justice flows down like rivers and righteousness like an ever-flowing stream. I invite you all to join in dreaming the birthing of a new church, for we need a shared vision, a bold vision and a transforming vision. *Dalitekklesia: A Church from Below* is one such offering towards that vision of transforming our world today.

I want to begin this conversation with the lyrics of a song that I wrote in my native language, Telugu, some twenty years ago as I began to develop my Dalit consciousness. You can listen to it on this link: https://soundcloud.com/commission-on-dalits-ncci/dalit-christmas-carol_telugu_o. This song speaks about the work of Jesus Christ in the lives of Dalit communities, my own personal testimony, which, in my view, sets the tone and rhythm for *Dalitekklesia,* a church from below.

Patta's Dalit Christian Telugu Song:

O Mallana O Maramma, mahithudu manishai vachenamma,

Masina brathukula nannitiki musi musi navvulu ichchenamma//

1.   *Ooru peru naku lekunna, ooruru ne thiruguthunna,*
     Oopiradani prajalaku, oorateda dorukunu ga,
     Oopiri posina devundu oorata ila galiginchenu ga
     //O Mallanna //

2.   *Meda midde naku lekunna, manasu ninduga nakunda,*
     Mosi mosi na brathukantha mosapothina jeevithamantha,
     Manalanu dari cherchina yesu, manashanthi ila ichchenu ga
     //O Mallanna //

3.   *Antarani vadanani dooram dooram chesiriga*
     Antithe avamanamani annitananu anagarchiriga
     Alpula kosam vachina yesu, aluperagaka nanu preminche
     //O Mallanna //

4.   *Avarnuniga ne nunna suvarnamuga chesenu yesa,*
     Anadhuniga ne nunna, sunadamutho nimpenu yesa,
     Alpula kosam vachina yesu, aluperagaka nanu preminche
     //O Mallanna //

English Translation

O Mallanna O Maramma (names of our Dalit Christian ancestors),
the God in the heavens has come as a human
To bring cheer and laughter to lives that have been called polluted

1.   *I did not have a place or name and have been wandering*
     place after place,
     For people without breath from where does comfort come
     from?
     God who has poured breath has granted comfort here and
     now

2. *Though I did not have a tower and a building, but I have a heart with contentment*
    Having carried and carried all my life, I was deceived all my life,
    Christ who has gathered us has granted us peace of mind and solace here and now.

3. *Because I was called untouchable, I was pushed far and far,*
    By touch they saw it as a disgrace and so they have oppressed me in all walks of life,
    Christ who has come for the last loved me tirelessly

4. *Though I was an outcast, Christ has transformed me as gold,*
    Though I was like an orphan, Christ has filled me with harmony
    Christ who has come for the last loved me tirelessly

PART I

The Locality of *Dalitekklesia: Peta*

This first part discusses the *Peta* (which in my language Telugu means locality, and is used for Dalit localities while upper caste localities are called *agraharam*), where *Dalitekklesia* happens.

Chapter 1

Can we Talk about Caste in our Church?

"Can we talk about caste in our church?" is the response I remember from a church member after listening to a sermon on a Dalit liberation Sunday in India. Have you ever heard a sermon about caste from your own pulpit? I remember that when I preached about the caste system that is deeply embedded in Indian society at an English service in Bangalore, the feedback I received was not to bring caste into the walls of the church, for it is not spiritual to talk about such issues. I was told that there were classrooms and newspapers for people to find out about issues of caste so much so that I had to ask, "Really?" When Indian society is defined by the caste system with so much justification around the division of society based on one's birth and labour, when caste is very much present within the Indian church, any talk or sermon about caste in the church gets silenced. Can we talk about caste in our churches? Perhaps the answer is, if we do not speak about caste, we are not living up to the calling of joining in Jesus in casting off the demons of our times. We should constantly speak about caste in our churches.

Here is a brief introduction about the understanding of caste. There are many theories around the origin of caste; however, I have chosen the perspective of Dr. B.R. Ambedkar, which is succinct and sets the tone in understanding caste for our context.

Caste is one of the oldest phenomena stratifying Indian society based on descent, occupation and colour. Its origins are traced back to Vedic history, associated with "the Aryan invasion," which according to the historian Romila Thapar, is claimed by many groups as the basis for their social and political roots.[1] The Aryan invasion of India took place over 3,000 years ago by the Indo-European-speaking people known as 'Aryans.' These people subjugated the indigenous people, the descendants of the land, and sanctioned their domination through the structure of the caste system, wherein people are divided into different strata. Louis Durmont observes, "The hereditary character of caste imposes a specific *dharma*—occupation to each *varna, or colour*, i.e. Brahmins as priests, Kshatriyas as warriors, Vaishyas as traders, and Shudras as servants."[2] Thus caste continued its dominance in Indian society, oppressing those born outside of the caste as 'untouchables.' Susan Bayly notes that caste enforced endogamy, dictated a hierarchical social division, and vested preferential economic and political power upon certain individuals, leading to the formation of divided social groups and varied cultural heritages.[3]

B.R. Ambedkar, the social revolutionary from the 'outcasted' community, contested caste, its structures and epistemology. He exposed the vested interests and the arrogance and selfishness of the caste system. In his paper "Castes in India, Their Mechanism, Genesis, and Development," which he read before the anthropology seminar of Dr. Goldenweiser on 9 May 1916, he has dealt with how and why the castes arose. According to him, the priestly class, to separate themselves from the other three classes for marriage, imposed the system of endogamy among themselves. This was separating a racially and culturally homogeneous people. The different racial groups—that is, the *Dravidians, the Scythians, and the Mongolians*—that had come to India from different directions, had forged cultural unity. The example of Brahmins was copied by the other classes. He has revealed that nobility imitates its leaders, its kings…, and … its nobility. The military classes, therefore, imitated the Brahmins, the highest caste, and the Vaishyas, the military classes. This is how classes, in due course, became castes.[4]

Ambedkar's address "Annihilation of Caste" contains a masterly analysis of castes, their weaknesses, disadvantages and harmful effects. Ambedkar says:

> There is no unanimity among the Vedas on the origin of *Varna Ashrama* (caste system). None of the other Vedas agree with the Rig-Veda that the four Varnas were created by Prajapati (literally means leader of people, here the divine). It does not mention which Prajapati, for there are so many Prajapatis in Hinduism. One says they were created by Brahman, another says they were created by Kassyaps, some say Manu. And even on the issue of how many Varnas, there is no unanimity. This chaos seems to be the result of concoction of the theory of *Chathurvarna* (four castes) which the Brahmins quietly singled into Rig-Veda contrary to established traditions.[5]

Ambedkar also says *"Purushasukta"* of the Rig-Veda is not a historical explanation. It is purely mystical. It is a fantastic dream of a troubled mind. It is probably an allegory, one which later Brahmins converted into a literal statement of hard fact. It does not solve the riddle; on the contrary it creates a riddle, which is why the Brahmins were interested in supporting the theory of *"Chaturvarna."*[6]

Thus, Ambedkar was very critical of the status quo of the caste system. To Ambedkar, there is no single origin of caste; it is always plural in number. When Brahmins made themselves a caste by enclosing themselves, they created the non-Brahmin caste and subsequently other social groups consolidated as closed social systems. Ambedkar criticises Western scholars' position of linking caste with colour. He says neither colour nor race has anything to do with caste.[7]

Exposing the various defences put forward to support the caste system, Ambedkar has stated that it is not only a division of labour but also division of labourers and that too on the basis of graded inequality. "Caste divides the labourers, caste disassociates work from interest, caste disconnects intelligence from manual labour and caste prevents mobilization."[8] Ambedkar has also criticised the Arya Samajists' theory of *"Chaturvarna,"* based on worth and not on birth, as impractical and difficult to achieve. He emphasises the need to reorganise the Hindu society on the principles of fraternity, liberty and equality in order to get away from the evil system of caste.

If we are committed to the Kingdom of God, if we want to follow Jesus Christ faithfully, and we remain silent about caste, it exposes our hypocrisy and our allegiance to the powerful. Jesus not only spoke about the structural injustice of his times but also healed and brought about a change in his society. If Jesus were to come to India today and to the diaspora communities across the world, Jesus would not keep silent about addressing the caste system; Jesus would have been at the forefront of any campaign or activity to address it. Dalit lives matter for Jesus. Join with Jesus in speaking and addressing caste in our churches today. The rest of the chapters provide an impetus towards that.

Endnotes

[1] Romila Thapar, "The Theory of Aryan Race and India: History and Politics," *Social Scientist* 24, no. 1/3 (1996), 28.

[2] Louis Dumont, *Homo Hierarchicus* (London: Paladin, 1972), 65

[3] Susan Bayly, *Caste, Society and Politics in India from the Eighteenth Century to the Modern Age* (Cambridge: Cambridge University Press, 1999), 13.

[4] D.K. Baisantry, *Ambedkar: The Total Revolutionary* (New Delhi: Segment books, 1991), 78.

[5] Vasant Moon, ed., *Dr. Babasaheb Ambedkar: Writings and Speeches Vol.4* (Bombay: Government of Maharashtra, 1987), 203-204.

[6] Ibid., 251.

[7] P. Mohan Larbeer, *Ambedkar on Religion* (New Delhi: ISPCK, 2003), 25-26.

[8] R. Sangeetha Rao, *Ambedkar on Varna, Caste and Class* (New Delhi: Sanjivayya Institute of Socio-Economic Studies, 1990), 10.

Chapter 2

The Locality of Dalit *Peta*: Mission Discourses

Introduction

"*28 States, 9 Union territories, 1618 Languages, 6400 Castes, 6 Religions, 6 Ethnic groups, 29 major Festivals & One country be proud to be an Indian. HAPPY INDEPENDENCE DAY.*" This was the greeting sent to me by a friend of mine on Indian Independence Day on the 15th of August. Yes, we are proud of our country for its rich and varied heritage and for the "unity in diversity" it maintains. But the most disturbing factor happens to be the composition of Indian society, which is marked by its caste stratification, with its deep roots in society. The 6,400 castes in India enjoy the benefits of power and dominion in the ladder of hierarchy in all walks of life, taking pride in their caste.

The grim reality in Indian sociology is the non-mention of a majority of people who live outside the purview of caste, who are treated as "outcastes," "Scheduled Castes," "no people," or "Dalits," and who constitute 16.6 per cent of the Indian population and live in *Peta, Cheri, Basti, Palle,* and so on. The busy Indian state and society are least bothered about the life and discrimination to Dalits who undergo and experience oppression in all arenas of life. For them, Dalits are a non-entity, and the entrenched belief is that one cannot change the fate of Dalits, who are born outside the divinely sanctioned caste system. The nature and substance of Indian society has not changed much, especially its caste-ridden roots even after 73 years of its political independence. Dalits and Adivasis in India are chained and oppressed in the name of caste and ethnicity. The modes and gravity of oppression today have only aggravated and in subtle, furious, heinous and crude ways. The socio-religious structures are so rigid that one is forced to succumb to and follow its ideology and way of life. The church in India is not an exception in maintaining the caste status quo in its pastoral and ministerial settings.

The question of what it means to witness Christ today certainly comes to the forefront; and in the Indian situation, mission as witness cannot but include the liberation of Dalits in its manifesto. When its caste roots define the context in India, what is mission today? Is justice to Dalits an important hermeneutical category in our missiological endeavours today? What has been the mission's approach to such an injustice done to Dalits in the name of caste in the history of missions in India? What is our theological direction in the ongoing journey of faith for the transformation of Dalit people? How can the church in India become a just and inclusive community? These are the few questions with which this paper would wrestle, attempting to bring out a few directions for a Dalit missiology for our times from the perspective of a young, Dalit, ecumenical learner. Exploring Dalit missiology is an offering of the Indian churches to the global theological enterprise, and the leads that emerge here will challenge and direct the mission agendas in our present contexts.

The Context of Dalit Realities

Every reality in context is dynamic and calls for creative responses in order to address those realities missiologically. Here is a brief description of Dalit realities from the standpoint of several vertices, which portray the Dalit predicament accordingly.

The Challenge of Dalit Oppression

The 3,000-year-old slavery of the so-called untouchable outcastes under Brahminical Hinduism has intensified the plight of the marginalised sections of Indian citizens who number about a quarter of the total population of India.[1] Dalits constitute 16.6 per cent of the Indian population, and are fettered by poverty and powerlessness. They are alien to freedom of the spirit. The oppressive and negative principle of hierarchy naturally denies any inherent equality of status to individuals or groups, particularly to vulnerable ethnic minorities like Dalits, and is against the divine imperative of creating all humans in the image and likeness of the Creator God. Their tears are never-ending and their humiliation knows no bounds.

On paper, untouchability is abolished in India, but in reality it is practised in every sphere of life. Imagine the pain of Dalits when they are called and treated as untouchables even in these postmodern days. "Untouchability in India is abolished, but not destroyed." The most frustrating concept in the lives of Dalits is the concept of 'purity' and 'pollution.' Dalits are the symbols of 'pollution' and hence untouchables.[2]

The Social Reality

Dalits in India are oppressed and wounded socially. Dalits are a social category and have been pushed into the peripheries and margins of society. With growing urbanisation, most Dalits are in exile in cities in search of jobs, but they have to settle with seasonal jobs, and most women are pushed into sex work to eke out a living.

> *In April 2007, in Bhandara district in Maharashtra, cow's urine was sprinkled on Dalit students by an upper caste teacher to purify them; for that teacher, cow urine is more purified than Dalits.*

Safai karamcharis (manual scavengers) in the community, who are involved in cleaning toilets, removing human excreta from dry latrines and cleaning septic tanks and sewages, are at the very bottom of the caste hierarchy; they also face discrimination from other Dalits who treat them as "untouchables," creating an unquestioned "'untouchability' within the 'untouchables….'" Manual scavenging is characterised by hazardous working conditions and health hazards. A manual scavenger from Paliyad village, Ahmedabad, Gujarat, described how in the rainy season:

> *"The water mixes with the faeces that we carry in baskets on our heads, it drips onto our clothes, our faces. When I return home, I find it difficult to eat food…. But in the summer, there is often no water to wash your hands before eating. It is difficult to say which [season] is worse."*[3].

The Political Reality

Dalits still do not have political freedom; exercising their franchise, contesting in elections and winning it has been tough. The Indo-Asian News Service (IANS) reported that on 6 August 2006, seven Dalit women from a village in Bihar were allegedly raped at gunpoint by upper caste landowners for refusing to vote for an upper caste landowner's wife in the local elections.

Violence and intimidation are also used to prevent Dalits from standing for election.

> *In October 2005, a Dalit woman, Prabhati Devi, was burned alive for contesting a panchayat (village council) election against an upper-caste candidate in Mirzapur district in Uttar Pradesh in defiance of a local politician's warning not to contest.*[4]

The slogan in politics is *"Vote caste, not cast vote."* Recently in Tamil Nadu, a Dalit panchayat post was auctioned for Rs. 2.5 lakh. The upper castes would rule the village while the Dalit panchayat president remained a rubber stamp.

The Violent Reality

Violence has been a continuous phenomenon on Dalits in India. Every day newspapers carry reports of incidents of violence against Dalits in every corner of India.

> *On February 04, 2007, a Dalit youth had to pay with his life for praying at a Shiva temple, antagonising the higher-caste Hindus. While Radheshyam Jatav (26) was offering prayers at the temple at Dahapura village near Nayagaon in Bhind district, Dashrath Rathore reached there and prevented him from offering prayers. Radheshyam, who was severely beaten up and kicked, was admitted to a private hospital at Gwalior, where he died on Thursday. Police said the postmortem report was awaited, while the accused was absconding.*[5]

Another grave incident, which depicts the crude forms of violence against Dalits, is the Khairlanji incident.

> *On September 29, 2006, returning home from a day's work in his field, Mr. Bhaiyalal Bhotmange, a Dalit, saw a mob going towards his house in the village Khairlanji in Maharashtra's Bhandara district. He saw people dragging out his wife, Mrs. Surekha, 40, two sons, Sudhir, 21, who was partially blind, and Roshan, 19, and daughter Priyanka, 17. The mob allegedly stripped the victims, and assaulted them with axes and other weapons and killed them. The*

bodies were loaded on to a bullock cart and dumped in a canal near the village. Horrifying as the events of September 29 were, what followed was even worse. The lack of response from the police who were informed when the massacre was taking place and the inept handling of the post-mortem by the medical personnel of the four Dalit persons who were killed all added to the advantage of the brutality of the oppressive upper castes.

Two Dalit youth were killed for winning cricket matches in Santagarh village in the district of Saharanpur in Uttar Pradesh by upper caste Rajputs, who charged them with theft in a village near Saharanpur.[6]

There are ample examples of atrocities on Dalits in India and these are just the tip of the iceberg. Violence is on the rise and has been crude. Incidents abound of Dalits being brutally beaten up by the upper caste mob. But who cares how many bones are broken and what is their physical health? There are incidents where Dalit women are raped inhumanly by as many as 10 persons. For the upper caste man, this may be a matter of heroism, but who cares for these women? Besides the mental and psychological torture they undergo, the physical pain is unimaginable. Their pain cannot be expressed and the wounds of untouchability are so sore that on every occasion, the tears flow and the wound bleeds.

The Economic Reality

Dalits have been the worst victims of globalisation in India. Multinationals seek profit at any expense and recruit only those with technical know-how, an affected accent and a fair complexion; Dalits rarely meet their requirements. Dalit farmer suicides are on the rise for they have huge debts with no price for their produce. Private employers routinely discriminate against Dalits, both in hiring and in the payment of wages. This discrimination is felt acutely by Dalit women.

> *The Untouchability in Rural India survey revealed that in 36 percent of the villages studied, Dalits were denied wage-paid employment in agriculture and in one-third of the villages were excluded from construction labour on the grounds that upper-caste community members did not want Dalits to "pollute" their homes. In 25 percent of the villages, Dalits received less than the market wage rate for their labour.*

According to the National Campaign for Dalit Human Rights (NCDHR), "untouchability" was also practised in the payment of wages such that "Dalits received wages in cash or kind from a respectable distance so that physical touch of a Dalit was avoided." Even well-educated Dalits are not immune from discrimination by private employers.[7] The present Government of India recently asked the Confederation of Indian Industry (CII) to give special training to Dalits and give them jobs in their industries to enhance their economic status. This special training has been advertised as the commitment to charity for Dalits while industries keep swindling Dalit land and natural resources. This too becomes a charade as they put several eligibility criteria to even be considered for training. On the other hand, the government has also come up with Special Economic Zones (SEZ) for private industries on lands from where Dalits and Tribals were forcefully evicted and displaced.

The Unhealthy Reality

Along with the wounds of untouchability, Dalits are prone to further injuries in terms of health. Dalits, who constitute 16.6 per cent of India's population, are subject to abject poverty, leading to poor health arising from social and economic discrimination and inhuman treatment for centuries. Statistics reveal that half of India's Dalit children are undernourished,

21 per cent are "severely underweight," and 12 per cent die before their fifth birthday.[8] The socio-economic conditions that Dalits live in make them a high HIV risk group. Living in drought conditions forces them to migrate in search of work, exposing them to HIV infections. With greater mobility, different categories of people have begun to run a higher risk of contracting HIV infection. Sexual exploitation by dominant caste males, forced prostitution—making Dalit girls temple prostitutes—high level of seasonal migration, and poverty and malnutrition are some of the realities that the community has to live with. Official records do not reveal the social background of the infected population. Going by their vulnerability, Dalits and Adivasis could be the largest section of victims. Moreover, Dalit males, who migrate seasonally to urban areas, increasingly contract HIV. [9] The humiliation of Dalits who become PLWHA (People Living with HIV/AIDS) knows no bounds. The stigma attached to HIV/AIDS, added to untouchability, makes HIV positive Dalits the worst affected.

The health condition of Dalit women is alarming, with high incidence of maternal mortality and infant mortality rates. This is because Dalit women are unable to access healthcare services. Owing to denial and sub-standard healthcare services, the life expectancy of Dalit women is as low as 50 years. The infant mortality rate is 90/1,000. The sex ratio of Dalit women is 922 per 1,000 males compared with 927 for the rest of the population in India. Due to poverty, Dalit women are malnourished and anaemic. Early marriage and multiple childbirths cause women to suffer from prolapsed uterus. Continuous bending and working while sowing and harvesting in agriculture cause acute back pain. They also develop skin irritation and allergy due to excessive use of pesticides. As they work barefoot in damp and wet soil, sores develop between their toes. Due to lack of awareness and medical care, many of them suffer from reproductive health complications, including STDs and cervical cancer. Dalit women are easy targets for government birth control schemes. Women face forced sterilisation and, like guinea pigs, are tested for the use of new invasive hormonal contraception. They are forced to use long-acting, hormonally dangerous contraceptives. They do not get basic medical facilities. Pregnant Dalit women receive discriminatory treatment in hospitals and there are instances where doctors have refused to conduct the delivery of Dalit women.[10]

A survey on human development by the National Council of Applied Economic Research reveals the spatial disparity in access to healthcare and safe drinking water. According to the survey, while 22 per cent of the villages have a healthcare centre (sub-centre) within the village, only 18 per cent of Dalit villages (a village predominantly having Dalit population—here the survey again does not seem to address residential segregation) had healthcare centres within the village. Similarly, for access to safe water, 60 per cent villages were covered by protected water sources in rural areas, but only 46 per cent of Dalit villages had that provision. The problems faced by Dalits in the rural areas originate from factors like physical isolation, low social capabilities, and lack of public services.[11]

The socioeconomic status of the health worker can also be a barrier to access.

> In three multi-caste villages in Pauri Gharwal, India, vaccination sessions were organized at the house of a local woman belonging to a high caste. Scheduled Caste women and their children were denied access to the house until the children of all the higher caste women had been vaccinated.[12]

With regard to manual scavenging, the safai karamcharis' exposure to raw sewage, which includes toxic industrial wastes, makes their work extremely hazardous. They suffer from tuberculosis, respiratory diseases, urinary tract infections, a range of skin diseases, eye disorders, gastrointestinal ailments, and even lung cancers. Thousands die every year while performing these tasks, but it evokes little public concern—the scavenger and the sanitation worker have ceased to be human for us.[13]

The Cultural Reality

Culturally and religiously, Dalits have no freedom in affirming their own cultural and religious values. When they do so, they are called either 'uncultured' or 'uncivilised.' Dalit arts and folk music are treated as outdated and not creative. Dalits are routinely prevented from taking part in religious and cultural rituals and festivals, with clashes ensuing if they choose to disobey the prohibition. The various ways in which wedding ceremonies are circumscribed are illustrative of such prohibitions; Dalit bridegrooms are not permitted to partake in the wedding tradition of riding a mare through the village, and Dalit weddings, in general, must be performed very quietly, without the public pomp and processions that usually accompany upper caste weddings.

> The Untouchability in Rural India survey found that out of the villages surveyed, a ban on marriage processions on roads was in place in 47.4 per cent of villages, while a ban on festival processions on public roads was in place in 23.8 per cent of villages.[14]

Also, while you may not believe that the Devadasi system (temple prostitution) exists even today, it is a reality.

The Dalit Christian Reality

The church in India, which is predominantly Dalit, has excluded the Dalit reality from their missional agenda. The Dalit issue has been a non-issue and the church in India has been insensitive to the Dalit cause all along. Christians from Dalit backgrounds have had to bear the brunt of indifference and ill treatment from three quarters:

- The hostile Indian public

- Unfriendly and arrogant upper caste Christians

- The rich and individualistic Christian missions

And, therefore, Dalit Christians are alienated, humiliated and marginalised thrice:

- By the hostile Hindu society

- By the unfriendly government

- By the unredeemed caste-minded Christian community

The following incident of discrimination against Dalit Christians reveals the dire reality of Dalit Christians in India:

The Dalit Christians in Erayur village of Villipuram district of Tamil Nadu, who were on an indefinite fast against the discrimination in their Parish by the Vanniyars, a caste group within the Church, were badly attacked and their homes were ransacked on the 9th March 2008. Two Christians died and many more wounded in police firing, as the police intervened to stop the clashes between the two communities within the Church. The violence was a fall out of a longstanding dispute over the rituals in the Church, for the Dalit Christians have been demanding equal rights in conducting the rituals to them. The Dalit Christians in Erayur have been demanding a separate parish in the diocese, and [it] has been a demand for several years now. The Dalit Christians in Erayur are forbidden to take their death or marriage processions to the Church through the main road, and instead the caste people have compelled the Dalit Christians to take a narrow road.[15]

Is this incident not disheartening, disturbing and disgusting? Indian Christianity in general and the Indian church in particular, with its deeply-rooted caste practices, have fallen prey to the gamut of discrimination at the expense of the gospel of Jesus Christ, which is love and liberation.

Here I would like to draw attention to the exclusion and marginalisation of Dalit Christians in three phases.

Exclusion and marginalisation of Dalits by Christian missions
Christianity was liberative to most Christians during the missionary movement, thanks to their tireless efforts in proclaiming the gospel. But a critical look will reveal the Christians mission's exclusivist attitude towards Dalits.

- Christian missions were keen on converting upper castes like Brahmins and Vellalas. By these upper caste conversions, they thought it would be easy to convert others, because of the influence upper castes had on them. The missionaries used strategies such as accommodation, adoption, 'Rigour of Mercy', and so tolerated the caste system within.

- Christian missions viewed high caste converts with favour and esteem, while their attitude towards Christians from Dalit backgrounds was indifference. The relationship between Christian missions and Dalits was like that of a giver and a receiver, patron and client. There was no equal footing for Dalits with other Christians because of their poverty; equality and justice were never emphasised and, at the most, the Dalit issue was a matter of charity.

- Only when the upper castes disappointed them did Christian missions turn to Dalit people through mass conversion. So, it was not a deliberate choice to come to Dalits, but a stepmotherly love towards Dalits.[16]

Exclusion and marginalisation of Dalits by the Indian church
The Indian church, which has to preach and practice the gospel of equality and liberation, has neglected to address the caste system within the church and has excluded Dalits.

- Dr. B.R. Ambedkar, the messiah of modern Dalit movement in India and the architect of the Indian Constitution, said: "Christianity has not succeeded in dissolving the feeling of caste from among the converts of Christianity. The Church school may be open to all. Still there is no gainsaying the fact that caste governs the life of Christians as much as it does the life of the Hindus. There are Brahmin Christians and non-Brahmin Christians. Among non-Brahmin Christians there are Maratha Christians, Mahar Christians, Mang Christians, Bhangi Christians, Pariah Christians, Mala Christians and Madiga Christians. They would not inter-marry, they would not inter-dine. They are as much caste ridden as the Hindus are." Dr. Ambedkar did not join Christianity because he saw caste system being visibly practised in the church and felt that Christians were self-centred.

- Besides such a practice, there are churches in India that do not accept Dalit pastors for non-Dalit congregations, or, for instance, a Mala Pastor for a Madiga community in Andhra Pradesh. It is a matter of shame to see separate cemeteries for Dalits and non-Dalits.

- As for the church leadership in India, most of it is with non-Dalit Christians. In one particular Church, two-thirds of the members were Dalits, but only 3.5 per cent of the priests were Dalits and no Dalit was consecrated as a bishop until 1993. In another big Church in India, of 150 bishops, only 10-15 are Dalits and Adivasis.

- The cruel fact is that caste priests often get posted to lucrative urban parishes, whereas Dalit priests and pastors are appointed in rural areas.

- The church also tries to create a 'Dalit Christian Middle Class' mentality so that Dalits are satisfied with second-class jobs. And even though there are Christian institutions and hospitals, there are no special reservation for Dalit Christians or Dalits in them.

- There is also a great struggle among Dalits who convert to Christianity to relate with their own community members because the church puts a barrier between their kith and kin who are non-Christians by preaching that they are no more people of darkness.

- For Dalit Christians, their identity is at stake. Dalits who convert to Christianity do not get equal status in the church with others; at the same time they lose the privileges due to them because they are Christian.

- Churches take 'Dalits' for granted. There is a neglect in pastoral care and counselling for Dalits in times of oppression and atrocities and insufficient attention to their ministerial, ritual and emotional needs.

- There is no space and participation for Dalit youth to be creative within the church, and unfortunately the church is not able to harness the potential of the youth.

Exclusion and marginalisation of Christians from Dalit background by the Indian state

Dalit Christians today form 1.3 per cent of the total population of India and have been denied their constitutional rights by the Indian state for the past seven decades. The struggle is on, and Dalit Christians and Dalit Muslims are waiting for justice to be done soon. As many as 85 per cent of Dalit Christians continue to live in the same *cheri* or colony or slum even two generations after becoming Christians. The humiliation and marginalisation continue, for we work in the same village for the same wages and the same masters, enduring the same tyranny, abuse, beating and killing. Except for the (wrong) records in the revenue offices, Dalit Christians are Dalit in every sense of the word, viz., ethnically, lineally, racially, socially, economically, culturally, vocationally, geographically, relationally, contextually and emotionally.[17]

- The 1950 Presidential Order of the Indian Constitution deprives justice and equal rights to Dalits who got converted to Christianity and Islam by denying them the Scheduled Caste status, unlike Dalits who were converted to Hinduism, Buddhism and Sikhism.

- The Indian government appointed a National Commission on Linguistics and Religious Minorities (NCRLM), headed by Justice Ranganath Mishra, in 2004 to study the backwardness of Dalit Christians and Muslims, and the commission has submitted its report to the Prime Minister's Office in Delhi. The Commission has recommended that extending Scheduled Caste privileges should be delinked from religion. The Commission report was recently tabled in Parliament after intense lobbying by the National Co-ordination Committee for Dalit Christians (NCCDC), a joint programme of the National Council of Churches in India (NCCI) and the Catholic Bishops' Conference of India (CBCI). So far, the government has not given a report on the actions taken based on the NCRLM report.

- There is a Public Interest Litigation (PIL) filed in the Supreme Court seeking justice for Dalit Christians, and the hearing is on with the Supreme Court giving time to the Centre to report on the status of the NCRLM report. It has already been two years since, with the Central government delaying its reply to the court.

Analysing the Dalit Reality in Our *Petas*

Having posited briefly on the ground reality of the Dalit situation in India, we will move on to several issues that arise as we churn through for our theological enterprise. This is not an exhaustive analysis but brings out certain signposts in our theologising today.

- As every reality or reality in context is dynamic and keeps changing accordingly, so also should our theological response to such realities be, with dynamism and creativity. Theologies can never enjoy the status quo but have to be thoroughly challenged and confronted by the dynamic realities around us. Dalit oppression has changed and perhaps has become more intense and subtle over the years; therefore new strategies, methodologies, tools and reflections need to evolve in order to make our theology relevant and vibrant. Theology should be more youthful.

- The realities around us support and clarify faith and, in return, faith should strengthen our commitment to addressing those realities.

- The realities need to be addressed holistically and not in isolation.

- In the context of socio-economic, political, violent and cultural oppression against Dalits, new means and mechanisms of pastoral care have to be developed. Ministry and mission need to be revisited to suit the reality of Dalits.

- Time has come now for the churches in India to confess and repent for their insensitivity to the Dalit cause and for its unchristian practices within the church. The church has to come forward reinvigorated with much spirit and energy to 'be a church for our times.'

- Public witness, people's empowerment, perspective building, political engagement and partnership can be added to the curriculum for theology today.

- It is only either caste or Christ that should exist in church and theology; if caste, then no Christ, and if Christ, then no more caste—this needs to be emphasised in our Christian nurture.

- The society, the church, the theologies and the texts need to be interpreted from the perspective of justice, equality and dignity.

- Since the church has not given them their space and have not taken their hopes and aspirations seriously, most Dalit Christian youth are moving towards secular Dalit movements, and the church has been a silent spectator to this exile.

Hermeneutical Categories in Missiological Discourse

On analysing the locality of Dalit *Peta*, one can decipher certain pertinent issues concerning mission in the missiological discourse. There are several trajectories that arise from these vertices of Dalit realities. In order to draw the parameters for mission from the perspective of Dalits, we need to locate these contextual realities in the integrated theology of mission enterprise. Therefore, in order to situate these realities in the context of mission discourse, the following five missional issues have been identified, which overarch the discussion of the Dalit context and provide a key to interpret the issues in the discussion of mission today.

    a.   Violation of *imago Dei*

    b.   Violence of indignity

    c.   Virulent injustice

    d.   Vicious oppression

    e.   Validity of a liberating church

Violation of *imago Dei*

Discrimination done to Dalits in the name of caste can be summarised as a grave violation of the *imago Dei*, the image of God, which has been given to all human beings equally. When God created all human beings in the entire history of humanity in God's own image, how can the inhuman caste system discriminate human beings in the name of caste and create a hierarchy in the image of God? Does an upper caste person have more *imago Dei,* and the person born outside caste a lesser *imago Dei*? If that is so, the meaning of *imago Dei* ceases to be the real image of God. "The *imago Dei* echoes the human worth of every individual, group, community, society and nations within and between. If this moral principal is fractured and fragmented, then the *missio Dei per se* becomes redundant, because in the process, its very essence, the *imago Dei,* is lost."[18] Therefore the basic missional issue that confronts Dalit struggles is the violation of the *imago Dei,* and therefore calls on the mission discourse to address this violation in its discussion.

Violence of Indignity

"Violation by and violence from the caste communities are the twin realities that Dalits encounter in their liberative journey... violence is unleashed on Dalits for any infracting of the prescriptions laid down for the caste-based hierarchical social order."[19] Violence against Dalits is one of the subtle and aggressive forms of discrimination against Dalits in our present times. Violence against Dalits is as old as caste discrimination itself; however, its present forms inflict insulting injuries both to the body and the psyche of Dalits. Violence against Dalits reveals its powerlessness and vulnerability in several spheres of life. Caste groups try to demoralise the spirit and aspirations of Dalits by creating a violent atmosphere, ostracising them morally and physically. The violence of indignity is so sore that no bandage can heal such a wound. Dalit women are beaten up and raped, but such news goes unnoticed and unheard by the authorities as caste groups are economically powerful. In such conditions, their dignity as humans is at stake and their identity as humans is lost. Therefore, violence against Dalits constitutes an important hermeneutical category to inquire into the framework of mission and the theology of mission.

Virulent Injustice

Dalits have been among the worst victims of injustice in human history. Scores of life realities depict the victimhood of Dalits caused by the injustice of caste. "The absence of justice is the source of all problems…. Dalits are denied justice, even legal justice, protection, assistance, education, healthcare and any possibility of mobility. For centuries they have been victims of aggression, rape, assault, scorn and rejection. Threats to survival, a stigmatised identity and a state of utter powerlessness are the main features of Dalit predicament. The backward castes too share the same at varying degrees. This reveals that caste is one of the key social mechanisms through which this sort of social and economic injustice is sustained in India."[20]

The injustice against Dalits has been powerful; it further drowns Dalits in the strong currents of discrimination while the caste groups, the perpetrators of this injustice, enjoy the privileges of the unjust practices in a society directed by market and consumerism. Dalits in India cannot enjoy the religious freedom guaranteed by the Constitution of India; if they choose to convert according to their freedom to Christianity and Islam, they lose their privileges and therefore become victims of injustice. Their long struggle for justice has been unheard and unaddressed for the past several years. "Justice delayed is justice denied, and justice denied is justice destroyed." Therefore, the virulent injustices on Dalits today is a hermeneutical category to address in the dialogue on mission.

Vicious Oppression

Dalits have borne the brunt of caste discrimination and have been lost in a whirlpool of oppression for years. From 'two-tumbler' experiences and cleansing by cow's urine to brutal rapes and cold-blooded murders, the vicious cycle of oppression is so grim that their struggles and pains know no bounds. "Dalit women are the victims of the unholy alliance of patriarchy, caste system and capitalism and their life is characterised by subordination, violence, drudgery and sexual exploitation."[21]

Besides caste, layers like patriarchy and globalisation add fuel to the fire of oppression of Dalits. With the advent of globalisation, Dalits have been pushed further away to the peripheries of society and are treated as non-entities in society. Dalit farmers' suicides are on the rise, and displacement of Dalits, underemployment and unemployment of Dalit youth aggravate the oppression of Dalits. One cannot sidetrack the oppression propagated through the written traditions, portraying Dalits as negative characters and by affirming their inferiority. Therefore, the vicious oppression with its several layers can serve as a hermeneutical lens for the missiological discourse.

Validity of a Liberating Church

At the crossroads of discrimination against Dalits, the church in India, as an important faith-based constituency, cannot shy away from the pertinent question, "Can caste and untouchability be abolished in all forms in the church?" The Indian church, irrespective of denominations and regions, has been equally culpable, along with the functionaries of the Indian state and society, in promoting and nurturing the ethos of caste and sub-caste within its jurisdictions. This question calls for a *metanoia* of the church from within.

It is an unfortunate fact from history that the church, as the powerhouse of the gospel of Jesus Christ and a means for liberation and freedom, has been caught up with caste and has fallen prey to its awkward, inhuman hierarchical intricacies. In one of the hearings on the long-pending Public Interest Litigation in the Supreme Court of India with regard to the Scheduled Caste status to be given to Christians of Dalit origin, the Chief Justice of India, Justice K.G. Balakrishnan, on 20 July 2007 raised a question, "Would the Christians admit that they practise caste system and that the Dalits among them face social discrimination requiring reservation to uplift their cause? This is not all that easy." [22]

To this startling question, I am not sure what the church and its leadership would answer. But I have heard many church heads pronouncing that "in Christ, there is neither Jew, nor Greek, neither master nor slave, neither male nor female, for all are one in Christ." This is a smart way of evading the problem. Theologically yes, the church should not practice caste, but praxiologically there exists a wide gap between objectivity and reality. Therefore, the validity of a church, which is liberating, can direct the mission discourse towards a transforming community.

Towards a Dalit Missiology

Having discussed the context of Dalit realities and then the hermeneutical categories in missiological discourse, we now try to attempt to bring out 'mission from the perspective of Dalits.' According to M.E. Prabhakar:

> *"Mission and ministries among Dalits, in particular, should then become directed towards interpreting God's liberating presence in a society that constantly denies to them their humanity, socially ostracises them, economically exploits them, culturally subjugates them, and politically marginalizes them and to seek justice and*

righteousness in that society for establishing true community, peace and harmony undergirded by the values of equality, liberty and fraternity."[23]

Therefore, the primary task of Dalit missiology is to interpret God's liberating presence in a society that oppresses and discriminates Dalits and to seek justice and righteousness in establishing a true community governed by equality, liberty and fraternity. God's liberating presence is omnipresent and the challenge, therefore, is to translate such a presence to the torn and struggling Dalit community, and that is possible when an individual experiences that liberating presence from within and communicates such an experience to all those who are oppressed.

According to David J. Bosch:

"Missiology, as a branch of the discipline of Christian theology, is not a disinterested or neutral enterprise; rather it seeks to look at the world from the perspective of commitment to the Christian faith. Such an approach does not suggest an absence of critical examination; as a matter of fact, precisely for the sake of the Christian mission, it will be necessary to subject every definition and every manifestation of the Christian mission to rigorous analysis and appraisal."[24]

Therefore, in attempting Dalit missiology, the basic factor that supervises the Dalit missiological rumination is the critical examination of the world from the perspective of Dalit realities and from the commitment to the Christian faith. The context of Dalit realities has already been analysed earlier, and that will provide the direction for Dalit missiology.

The Rationale

Why Dalit Missiology? Is the mission understanding that exists today not sufficient to address the concerns and issues of Dalits? What is the rationale for such a Dalit missiology? The answers to these questions will certainly provide certain signposts in the onward journey of Dalit missiology.

- Dalit missiology is the result of Dalit theology, addresses dire Dalit concerns from a missiological point of view, and tries to transform the society into a new community that is just and inclusive, free from all caste and discrimination. Therefore, Dalit missiology is the need of the hour.

- The existing missiology in India has been borrowed from Western missiological endeavours, be it the methodology or mission analysis. And, therefore, caste analysis may not find space in its methodology. The present missiology in India addresses a broad spectrum of issues, including religious pluralism, ecumenism, wider ecumenism, ecological concerns, and so on. Its limit and scope is too vast to address all these varied issues, and so a Dalit missiology is required to keep alive the hopes and aspirations of the crushed Dalit people and that which can provide theological and missiological tools and lenses to deal with the Dalit predicament in the Indian scenario more effectively and creatively. Though the Dalit issue is interrelated to other mission issues, Dalit missiology attempts to prioritise Dalit concerns and would discuss other related issues from the perspective of Dalits, rather than discussing the Dalit issue from other mission-issue perspectives.

- It has been nearly four decades since Dalit theology has taken its shape and form. Ever since the first theological explorations from Dalit perspective began, there have been several distinguished Dalit theologians who have attempted theologising on several aspects and facets of Dalit theology. Thanks to all those theologians for their profound contributions to the Dalit theological enterprise, Dalit theology, Dalit Christology, Dalit pneumatology, Dalit hermeneutics, Dalit ecclesiology, Dalit philosophy and Dalit ethics have all been attempted and they have influenced the church and academy in participating in a transforming community. All these facets in Dalit theology have latently addressed the mission aspect within their theological articulations. However, there have been no academic, theological or systematic reflections on Dalit missiology. Therefore, such an attempt would be a first of its kind, and would add yet another feather in the cap of the Dalit theological enterprise.

- The rationale for Dalit missiology is to interpret the liberating presence of God among Dalit communities and to communicate the gospel of salvation through Jesus Christ among Dalit communities and to establish a society with justice, peace and equality.

- In all the mission endeavours, there has always been a danger in making Dalits and Dalit communities objects of mission and not subjects of mission. Mission 'to' Dalits was more emphasised over the years. Therefore, the rationale for Dalit missiology is that it falsifies all treatises and practices objectifying Dalits and emphasises a mission from and at the margins.

- Dalit missiology is directed towards a theology of life for all and is not parochial in its outlook. Therefore, such a missiology can take into consideration the oppressions and modern forms of slavery and shall provide a method in addressing all such practices aimed at transforming the whole of the community.

The Content: Mission in Christ's Way

The content of Dalit missiology would be in line with the struggle for justice from the standpoint of Jesus Christ. Missiology and Christology will go hand in hand and therefore Dalit missiology derives its content from the work of Christ. Mission in Christ's way revolves around the values of the reign of God, and it is a hard task to summarise the whole missional activity of Jesus Christ because of the limitation of time and space. Nevertheless, I would like to draw your attention to four sayings of Christ, and the reasons for his coming to this world, sent by God to fulfil the mission of God here on earth. These sayings will be the driving force for evolving Dalit missiology. Mission in Christ's way challenges all of us to become active agents of transformation, particularly in the transformation of Dalit lives.

"I must preach good news of the Kingdom of God to the other towns also, because that is why I was sent." Luke 4:43

Jesus Christ's coming into this world is to preach the good news of the reign of God to other people in other towns. Mission primarily is understood as evangelism, preaching the good news, and emphasis is laid on the Great Commission given by the resurrected Jesus Christ to his disciples in Matthew 28. Leaving aside all the controversies of the redaction criticism of the Matthew account, the focus of Dalit missiology is on Christ's mission, for he was sent to preach the good news of the reign of God. Mission for M.M. Thomas could be defined as the communication of the message of salvation through Jesus Christ to the end so that people may respond in faith and be saved. This is the cutting edge in mission. Mission is primarily an evangelical mission or a mission of salvation.[25] Salvation, according to Thomas, is the realisation of "the ultimate meaning and fulfilment of human life revealed in the divine humanity of the crucified and risen Jesus Christ."[26] This salvation has two directions. One is eschatological and the other is historical. Salvation remains eschatological, but the historical responsibility within the eschatological framework cannot but include the task of humanisation of the world in secular history.[27] Though these two are not identical, both have a deep nexus between them. Thomas says that salvation is the spiritual inwardness of true humanisation, and humanisation is inherent to the message of salvation.[28] Drawing relevance from Thomas' understanding of mission in our present discussion on Dalit missiology would then be to communicate the message of salvation/liberation/ transformation/humanisation through Jesus Christ, who was raised by God victoriously, breaking the chains of death and oppression to all people, particularly those who are dehumanised and subhumanised in the name of caste.

The other aspect in Christ's mission is to preach the good news to other neighbouring towns. This reveals the importance of **networking** of the good news among people in different towns and villages. Jesus' mission primarily was centred around rural villages and towns; therefore, when Dalits and Dalit struggles are the glaring reality of our towns and villages, the calling for Dalit missiology is to emphasise its locus in local areas in villages and towns and to strive to network with all like-minded movements working for the cause of liberation and transformation. Therefore, mission according to Christ's way is preaching the good news of the reign of God, networking with other people in neighbouring localities, and is a local initiative.

"*For judgement I have come into the world, so that the blind will see and those who see will become blind." John 9: 39*

Christ's way of missioning is not always soothing and of the armchair variety. Jesus Christ time and again confronted the oppressive forces of his day, and was bold in calling a 'spade a spade.' He did not mince words, but rather was prolific and prophetic in his missional approaches. There was aggression in Christ's words and actions, aggression for the sake of giving life to all. The present saying of Christ reveals a profound mission motive for coming into this world. Throughout mission history, Christians and missions were content with the preaching of the good news and interpreted it to the extent of giving charity to the poor and weak. Christian missions in India did not boldly preach and practice the virtues of justice, a transformative justice. This saying of Jesus Christ is a reminder to the missions today to be bold in preaching the judgement so that the blind will see and those who see will become blind.

The context in which Jesus uses these mission words is in the healing of a blind man, where the religious leaders condemn Jesus and his healing and the blind man too. Jesus, who came to give life in all abundance, makes sure that life is given at any cost, no matter the religious sanctions; texts and leaders try to limit it. Besides giving sight to the blind, Jesus also blinds the short-sighted, selfish and nominally religious people, for they try to obstruct healing to the oppressed. When Jesus says he has come to give "good news to the poor," have we ever translated that as "bad news to the rich?" I believe that is the strength of the good news, to convince the poor and to make the rich confess their greed and selfish motives. The theory of retribution will have its due place in Dalit missiology. "You will be paid for what you have done" and "you will reap the consequences right here in this world for what you have sown" provide ample space for missioning in the context of Dalits. Over the years, the preaching from the pulpit has been that one will be rewarded in life after death or accounted in the life after death, sidetracking the ontological relevance of Christ's mission. Therefore, this saying of Christ provides a clue in Dalit missiology to address the needs of the oppressed and the need for the oppressor to repent and face a tough judgement.

The international consultation on 'Dalit theology and a theology of the oppressed' held in Chennai in 2004 came out with a statement calling churches to develop a theology of liberation for the oppressor that would seek their repentance, reconciliation and removal of systemic and structural practices of caste. Therefore, mission according to Christ's way is to give sight to the blind and to call for reconciliation and repentance from the people who have been oppressing, for they will be judged accordingly.

"For I did not come to judge the world, but to save it." John 12: 47

The other facet in Christ's way of mission is that he has come to save the world and creation, which are groaning in bondage awaiting liberation. Jesus Christ's missional framework can be best understood in his messianic perspective. He has come to save people from all bondage and oppression. He has come to liberate all who are oppressed and his salvation implies a holistic one, liberation from all facets of sin and discrimination. "Jesus' whole life till his death on Cross is a complete manifestation of God's kingdom of love. In Jesus, God is the defender of the forgotten and the marginalized of the society. By receiving sinners and outcastes, by caring for Samaritans and Gentiles, and by defying the oppressive ways of observing Sabbath, he provokes the anger of the religious leaders. Jesus claims that his mission was to seek the lost, the least and the rejected."[29] Therefore Jesus' mission primarily was to save and love those lost in society.

Jesus Christ came to this world to save the world from both individual and corporate sins. "Spiritual ignorance, moral depravity, intellectual dishonesty, social oppression, economic exploitation, etc., all are the manifestations of sin,"[30] and therefore Christ's way of mission is to save the world from these manifestations of sins. Christ came to this world to save, liberate and transform the world to make it a place free from all evils and vices. He came to "bring good news to the poor, give sight to the blind, release the captives, set at liberty all that are oppressed and to proclaim the liberating year of the Lord," and so was his mission. Jesus Christ fulfilled the mission mandate he set before his ministry and therefore calls on Dalit missiology to have such a mandate and agenda in its directions and messages.

"In fact, for this reason, I was born, and for this I came into this world, to testify to the truth." John 18: 37

Another of Jesus Christ's reason for coming to this world, the reason for his mission, was to testify to the truth in this world. Jesus Christ provides the clue to the truth, for in knowing the truth one is liberated. Truth is not one's exclusive property, and therefore Jesus' way of mission is to testify to the truth, the truth of liberation and the truth of equality. Since God is truth, as the mission agent sent from God, Jesus Christ testifies to the truth and provides the way towards the truth, for he leads everyone to truth from all falsehood. Situating this missiological approach of testifying to the truth within the parameters of Dalit missiology, the lessons to be drawn from this way of Christ's mission is to testify and witness to the truth of equality, freedom, justice and peace. Testifying to the truth is condemning the falsehood of caste and the inequality it promotes and to live by the truth, for the truth is liberating. Witnessing (*marturia*) to the truth is to become a martyr for the cause and sake of the truth, which is all liberating. Therefore, Dalit missiology calls for a mission paradigm that calls people to live in truth and to testify to the truth of liberation and life.

Mission as witnessing, mission as leading to all truth, and mission as confronting all falsehood provide the basis for an emerging Dalit missiological paradigm. Truth is always triumphant, and one who testifies to the truth is also triumphant and will emerge victorious from all pangs of bondage and oppression. So, Dalit missiology leads Dalits into the truth and make them live in hope, for the truth is always victorious; liberation is not far when everyone lives in truth. Because of growing falsehood, there is more oppression and discrimination, for caste creates false apprehensions of inequality and unjust practices. Therefore, Christ's way of mission is to testify to the truth, to live in truth and make all live in truth. When truth overarches the society in which we live in, transformation is at hand.

The Directions: Mission Today

With the characteristics mentioned above, particularly the hermeneutical categories discussed, and with the content tracing from Christ's way of mission, I would like to bring in a tentative direction here, suggesting rather than defining the contours of Dalit missiology. The discussions and suggestions below are neither exhaustive in nature nor live in isolation, for they are all integral to each other and complement each direction prescribed here. Here are five tentative suggested directions for Dalit missiology. Taking into consideration the paradigm shift from ecclesia-centric mission to Christo-centric mission to theo-centric (God-centric) mission, I propose five aspects of *missio Dei* in the Dalit missiological space.

Missio Dei as safeguarding the imago Dei

When the *imago Dei* of Dalits is fractured and destructed by the weapons of caste, *missio Dei* will be challenged, for the mission of God is to see to that the image of God is safeguarded in all human beings, in all histories. Jesus Christ's coming to this world is to restore and reclaim the lost image of God, destroyed by sin and disobedience. But caste and its ramifications have been distorting the equal image of God given to all human beings, for they have torn, blurred and shattered the image of God in the Dalit people. Therefore, the mission of God in a situation like this is to safeguard and protect the image of God in Dalits, for they are co-heirs along with Christ to the rich legacy of God and God's reign. "The life with God and *missio Dei* must offer the moral/spiritual power to heed to the vision of justice so that the *imago Dei* could be realised both at micro and macro levels."[31] If the image of God in Dalits is distorted, the image in God also is affected, and if the mission of God restores the image of God in Dalits, then the mission of God is fulfilled.

As Christ says that "he and his Father are one" in John 17, one can see the close relationship between 'being' and 'being sent.'[32] Therefore, when the image of the human being is distorted, the image of the being sent and the image of the being are shattered too. The images of God, Christ and humans continue to be sustained in all equality, and the role of the mission of God is to see to it that the three images of God in God, Christ and human will not be disturbed at any cost. This paves the method and direction for the Dalit missiological endeavour of our times.

Missio Dei as overcoming violence

The mission of God in the context of Dalit realities is to assist Dalits to overcome violence of all forms on them. Over the years, non-violence has been the method used by Dalits to overcome or confront violence. When violence was inflicted on Dalits, silent protests and peace marches were encouraged to address the violence done to them. This while the violent oppressors continued to attack, ostracise, rape and kill their kin. There was no support for Dalits in tackling the perpetrators of violence, for the authority, power and money lie in the hands of the upper caste.

The other option is violence as resistance to the violence done to Dalits, which is not new to Dalits. But, is violence an answer to violence? Can this be part of the mission of God in overcoming violence? In such a discussion on violence, Sathianathan Clarke's observations provides the context. He suggests: "…That victimised collectives such as Dalit communities can creatively work on means to use symbolic violence in proactive ways. This may be an acceptable method of preventive violence, one which can safeguard Dalits against the well-oiled wheels of fierce and vicious caste machine." He further proposes "rebounding violence' which does not instrumentalise violence, but adroitly deflects violence back to the originator."[33] Does this symbolic violence and rebounding violence suit the ambience of Dalit missiology and as an expression of the mission of God? In such a situation, Jesus Christ's mission comes to the rescue of our situation in overcoming violence. Jesus cleansing the temple, Jesus taking the whip, and Jesus pronouncing that he has not come to give peace but a sword provide enough basis for addressing violence through symbolic violence and rebounding violence.

Jesus Christ may not approve passive non-violence, for he never accepted the unjust status quo of his times. When Dalits are attacked, what legal safeguards are maintained? What justice do they receive? The mission of God is not a static, blind and lethargic one, rather it is a proactive and dynamic one, which addresses issues according to local requirements and situations. Therefore, the mission of God tries to see that violence in all forms is overcome and is taken to the right platforms for giving justice to the victimised Dalits.

Missio Dei as overcoming injustice

When injustices are rampant in Indian society, and when Dalits have to bear the brunt of it more than anyone else, what is the mission of God in such a situation? Jesus' Sermon on the Mount, particularly when he says, "Blessed are those who hunger and thirst for justice/righteousness for they will be filled" (Mat 5:6), has not taken deep roots in the ongoing faith journeys of Christians. Christians turn a deaf ear to such hunger and thirsts for justice and has conveniently used Christ's call to feed the people as a matter of charity. Therefore, the primary calling of the mission of God is to locate this saying of Jesus in the sociopolitical and economic context of Dalits and to translate this message of justice to Dalits as the prime mission goal. "The promised reign of God is a reign of justice for those who have been unjustly treated. It is a reign of compassion for those who have been fragmented, broken and injured; it is a reign of accountability for those who have wielded power; it is a reign and inclusion and solidarity for those who have been marginalized and excluded."[34]

Dalit missiology attempts to establish such a reign of God where the axis of life revolves around justice and peace. In the context of the injustice done to Dalit Christians for the past six decades in denying their rights, the mission of God is to strive for advocacy and lobby for their rights. Exerting pressure on the government should be part of the Christian calling as standing for justice is highly biblical and Christian. Empowering people is an important objective in achieving justice for Dalits. Empowerment is not something that comes from external forces, but it comes from harnessing the latent potential within Dalit communities and giving them enough information and awareness on their rights to get justice. A systemic analysis of the structured injustices needs to be done to make Dalit missiology more vibrant and creative. When God is just and righteous, the mission of the one sent is just and righteous, should not the mission today be just and righteous?

The mission of God as overcoming injustice is sustained by the 'Right to Information' revolution, for people are able to discern when information is given and is available for access. Therefore, the mission of God is to overcome injustice in all forms and natures.

Missio Dei transforms church to a just and inclusive community

'Is Church a just and inclusive community?' This question comes to the forefront in the missiological discourse, comes straight into the altars of our churches, to the pulpits of our churches, to the decision-making tables of our churches, to the Christian formation classes, to our daily devotions, to our worships and to all our lifestyles. Are we bold enough to answer this question? To the core of our consciousness, are we truthful to the Christian calling and the values of the gospel? What is our answer? If it is silence, beware such a silence at such a moment like this may turn to be violence against us, for our calling is to "abolish and destroy caste and untouchability at its roots." If we as church need to answer that caste is completely abolished for it is against the gospel, then we as church should be exemplary in our attitude, actions and affirmations.

"A people's concept of mission is about embodying Jesus Christ's gospel of justice, love and freedom. The challenge therefore is about becoming the real Church, the body of Christ—the broken body of Christ—the Church of the poor, Dalits and Tribals in India."[35] In order to become the real body of Christ, the church needs to come to grips with the mission of Jesus Christ so that it can practice equality and justice in all its ministries. A strong solidarity system needs to be put into place so that concerted social pressure continues to be exerted against those structures that sustain the injustices of caste. This will let the church become such a force of solidarity where caste is completely abolished, destroyed and uprooted from our churches, and pave the way for society to feel the strength of leaven in the church. The church needs to be an open community, a church without walls, a church with all inclusivity and a church where no discrimination and divisions have a place; such a church will be the sign of the coming of the reign of God, and only then the church will exist for the people. Therefore, the mission of God is to transform the church as a counterforce, as a people's movement and as a community of all people of God, where peace, justice, equality and dignity are practised.

Conclusion

The discussion thus far has been an exhaustive one. However, in exploring the trajectories for a relevant Dalit missiology today, I believe the discussions above direct and lead us to crystallising the hypothesis. Dalits have been omitted in several phases of life and continue to live a life in oppression and discrimination. Their omission has challenged a redrafting of the mission mandate in the backdrop of justice, because they have been the worst victims of injustice in the twenty-first century. The church is commissioned to address their omission, and here is the outline for a Dalit missiology, which addresses the omission of Dalits and calls the church to "come-mission." The analysis of Dalit realities has been an exhaustive one that provides the base to build Dalit missiology for our times. Christ's mission way has been the influencing force in constructing Dalit missiology, for Christology, ecclesiology and missiology are all interconnected. If the being for a Dalit church is ecclesiology, the living for a Dalit church is Christology and the doing of a Dalit church is missiology. This is a humble effort, and I am sure will influence many young Dalit theologians and all people of God to participate in the Dalit mission of God by realising justice as the key component in their ongoing faith journeys.

Let me end with the words of Bishop Azariah, quoted from his famous speech at the 1910 Edinburgh Mission Conference. Bishop Azariah said:

> The exceeding riches of the glory of Christ can be fully realized not by the Englishman, the American, and the Continental alone, nor by the Japanese, the Chinese, and the Indians by themselves—but by all working together. Worshipping together, and learning together the Perfect Image of our Lord and Christ. It is only 'with all the Saints" that we can "comprehend the love

of Christ which passeth knowledge, that we might be filled with all the fullness of God.' This will be possible only from spiritual friendships between the two races. We ought to be willing to learn from one another and to help one another. Through all the ages to come the Indian Church will rise up in gratitude to attest the heroism and self-denying labours of the missionary body. You have given your goods to feed the poor. You have given your bodies to be burned. We also ask for love. Give us FRIENDS![36]

Dalit missiology is directed towards building friendships among all people of God. Let the Indian church and society transcend the boundaries of caste identities and let true friendship be built on the values of equality and justice. Dalits today seek friends who are willing to change the face of society from its caste-ridden roots to caste-free communities. May we all join together to participate in transforming the community, where justice, peace and equality will prevail and be sustained. Towards that direction, may God's faithfulness accompany all of us in our struggle for liberation.

Endnotes

[1] M. Azariah, "Ecumenism from the Perspective of the Marginalised," 205.

[2] K.M. Ziyauddin & S. Acharya Sanghmitra, *The Dalit Question: Some Concerns about Work and Health,* in www. ivcs.org.uk/ijrs/oct/2005.

[3] "Caste Discrimination against Dalits or so-called Untouchables in India: Information for the consideration of the committee on the elimination of racial discrimination in reviewing India's fifteenth to nineteenth periodic reports," presented at the Seventieth Session of the Committee on the Elimination of Racial Discrimination February 2007, prepared by the Center for Human Rights and Global Justice and Human Rights Watch., 56.

[4] Caste Discrimination against Dalits…, 44.

[5] http://www.rediff.com/news/2007/feb/09dalit.htm

[6] http://www.pucl.org/Topics/Dalit-tribal/2004/santagarh.htm

[7] Caste Discrimination against Dalits…, 60

[8] http://www.europarl.europa.eu/sides/getDoc.do?pubRef=-//EP//TEXT+TA+P6-TA-2007-0016+0+DOC+XML+V0//EN

[9] http://www.combatlaw.org/information.php?article_id=744&issue_id=28

[10] http://www.imadr.org/en/news/pdf/DALIT%20WOMEN%20CERD%20Report%20by%20TNWF.pdf

[11] S. Venkatesan, "Why Dalits Stay Poor in India," in http://southasia.oneworld.net/article/view/130516/1/1819

[12] http://whqlibdoc.who.int/bulletin/1999/Vol77-No9/bulletin_1999_77(9)_722-730.pdf

[13] Lalitha Jisnu, "One Million Salves – all Dalits," in *Invisible India* cited in www. businessworld.in/May3005/web_exclusive03asp.

[14] Caste Discrimination against Dalits...,66-67.

[15] *The Times of India*, 10 March 2008, 7.

[16] S. Manickam, "Mission's Approaches to Caste," in *Dalits & Women*, edited by V. Devasahayam, (Gurukul: Madras, 1992), 60-69.

[17] *Demand for Restoration of Equal Rights for Dalit Christians*, booklet by National Co-ordination Committee for Dalit Christians in 1997.

[18] I. John Mohan Razu, "Dalits–Tribals as Victims of Asymmetries: A Liberative Mission Perspective," in *Mission in the Past and Present: Challenges and Perspectives*, edited by Samson Prabhakar, (BTESSC/SATHRI: Bangalore, 2006), 74.

[19] Sathianathan Clarke, "Dalits Overcoming Violation and Violence, A Contest between Overpowering and Empowering Identities in Changing India," in *The Ecumenical Review*, Vol 54, no.3, July 2002, 291- 293

[20] Deenabandhu Manchala, "Mission as Struggle for Justice: From the Perspective of those who are denied Justice," in *Quest for Justice*, edited by George Mathew N. Nalunnakkal & Abraham P. Athyal, (ISPCK/NCCI/Gurukul: Delhi, 2000), 41-43.

[21] F. J. Balasundaram, "Set Us Free—A Cry of the Marginalised: Dalit Perspective," *NCCI Review*, Vol CXIX, no.4, April 1999, 291.

[22] *The Times of India*, 21 July 2007.

[23] M. E. Prabhakar, "Missions in a Dalit Perspective" in *Dalits & Women*, edited by V. Devasahayam, (Gurukul: Madras, 1992), 72.

[24] David Bosch, *Transforming Mission, Paradigm Shifts in Theology of Mission,* (New York: Orbis, 1991), 9.

[25] M.M. Thomas, *Salvation and Humanisation* (Madras: CLS, 1971), 2.

[26] M.M. Thomas, "The Meaning of Salvation Today," in *Towards a Theology of Contemporary Ecumenism*, 181.

27 M.M. Thomas, *Salvation and Humanisation*, 8.

28 Ibid., 10.

29 Deenabandhu Manchala, "Mission as Struggle for Justice: From the Perspective of those who are denied Justice," 46.

30 M. E. Prabhakar, "Missions' in a Dalit Perspective," 81.

31 I. John Mohan Razu, "Dalits–Tribals as Victims of Asymmetries: A Liberative Mission Perspective," 75.

32 Jan AB. Jongeneel, *Philosophy, Science, and Theology of Mission in the 19th and 20th Centuries*, (Peterlang: Frankfurt, 2002), 198.

33 Sathianathan Clarke, "Dalits Overcoming Violation and Violence, A Contest between Overpowering and Empowering Identities in Changing India," 296-98.

34 Richard Dickinson, "Economic Globalisation: Deepening Challenges for Christians" as quoted by Deenabandhu Manchala, "Mission as Struggle for Justice: From the Perspective of those who are denied Justice," 47.

35 George Mathew N. Nalunnakkal, "Mission as if People Mattered: An Indian Perspective," in *Re-routing Mission*, edited by George Mathew Nalunnakkal, (CSS: Tiruvalla, 2004), 106.

36 http://www.towards2010.org.uk/downloads/t2010mainintro.pdf

Chapter 3

Listening to Ambedkar at our *Peta:* Cast out Caste

Introduction

At most of our Dalit *wadas, cheris* and *petas,* the statue of Ambedkar finds a prominent place with the Constitution of India in one hand, while the other points towards the *peta.* The presence of Ambedkar in our localities—standing physically as a statue, ideologically as a reminder for us to educate, agitate and organise, and metaphorically as a sign of resistance to evil caste oppression—is an act of resilience for Dalit communities. As we discuss *Dalitekklesia,* the church in India has to listen to Ambedkar and his prophetic voice towards Dalit liberation. This chapter is an invitation to listen to Ambedkar and his analysis, for a church from below happens when Ambedkar becomes our conversant partner and his analysis becomes a rich resource in being and becoming a church relevant for our locality.

Down the lane of Indian history, one courageous man analysed the socio-religious structures of his day and challenged the oppressive nature they have and strived for the liberation of society. He is none other than the messiah of Dalits, Bharat Ratna Dr. Babasaheb Ambedkar. At the Golden Jubilee celebrations of Baba Saheb's *Dhamma Chakra Parivartan* (conversion to Buddhism), a question raised was, "How relevant is Ambedkar to the life of the church in India?" This question inspired me to reflect on Ambedkar's contributions, specifically his analysis of the Indian context. "The Indian society owes a tremendous debt to Ambedkar's radical and humanitarian approach for the solution of the problems of the backward classes," writes S.B. Chavan, the former Chief Minister of Maharashtra[1]. As a social reformer, Ambedkar ushered in a new era in India's sociopolitical history. On the very front page of his book *What Congress and Gandhi have Done to the Untouchables*, Ambedkar quoted the Greek philosopher Thucydides who said, "It may be your interest to be our master, but how can it be ours to be your slaves?"[2] Ambedkar was bold in questioning the validity of the caste system and made Dalits aware of their rights and duties. Ambedkar stood against religious oppression and embraced Buddhism so as to free his people from Brahminical subjugation. It is interesting to note that for him untouchability and exploitation were a violation of civil liberties not in the conventional sense, but because of the breach of the dignity of whole communities.

This chapter is an attempt to bring out Ambedkar's analysis of socio-religious structures of the then Indian society. His method of analysis was radical, reformatory and revolutionary. The Hindu social order, the caste system, the untouchability and the religion in which it was practised are all analysed and discussed here. The relevance of such an analysis to the theology of the church's ministries in India is also discussed here.

Analysis of Indian Society

Gail Omvedt writes: "It is impossible to conceptualize the Dalit movement in India in the absence of Ambedkar, it is equally difficult to imagine, sociologically, Ambedkar coming of any other region than the Marathi speaking areas of British presidency."[3] This is one of the reasons for Ambedkar's critical position on nationalist politics. He was a Mahar, the largest untouchable caste in Maharashtra. His actions were moulded not only by his own personal background, achievements and the Maharashtrian thinking of his day, but also by his status as an untouchable. This group he came from had begun social and political movements before he assumed a position of leadership.

Many communist leaders analysed caste in a mechanical framework and sought to override traditional identities rather than reinterpret them. Therefore, a plausible explanation can be found in his own solution for liberating Dalits. Ambedkar realised that the identification of Indian culture with Hinduism was incorrect. He saw the caste system as a serious obstacle in the path to democracy. According to him, democracy lies not in the form of government but in terms of association between the people who form that society. Because Indian society is divided and graded on the basis of the caste system it is not democratic.[4] He was critical of the Brahminical social order and put forward arguments based on the principle of liberal equality and distributive justice.

Analysis of Caste System

This devilish system is mainly responsible for the degradation of the untouchables. Dr. Ambedkar has, therefore, never spared himself from exposing the vested interests and arrogance and selfishness that have gone into creating this barrier, and the high-handedness in maintaining it. In his paper "Castes in India, their Mechanism, Genesis and Development," which he read before the anthropology seminar of Dr. Goldenweiser on 9 May 1916, he dealt with how and why the castes arose. According to him, the priestly class, to separate themselves from the other three classes in marriage, imposed the system of endogamy among themselves. This was parcelling of a racially and culturally homogeneous people. Different racial groups, that is, *Dravidians, Scythenians and Mongolians*, who had come to India from different directions had forged cultural unity. The example of the Brahmins was copied by the other classes. He has revealed that nobility imitates its leaders, its kings or sovereigns, and the people likewise, given the opportunity, its nobility. The military classes, therefore, imitated the Brahmins, the highest, and the Vaishyas the military classes. This is how classes, in the course of time, became castes.[5]

Dr. Ambedkar's address "Annihilation of Caste" contains a masterly analysis of castes, their weaknesses, disadvantages and harmful effects. Ambedkar says: "There is no unanimity among the Vedas on the origin of **Varna Ashrama** (four castes). None of the other Vedas agree with the Rig-Veda that the four Varnas were created by Prajapati. It does not mention which Prajapati, for there are so many Prajapatis in Hinduism. One says they were created by Brahman, another says they were created by Kassyaps, some say Manu. And even on the issue of how many Varnas, there is no unanimity. This chaos seems to be the result of concoction of the theory of **Chathurvarna,** which the Brahmins quietly singled into Rig-Veda contrary to established traditions."[6] Ambedkar also says the *"Purushasukta"* of Rig-Veda is not a historical explanation. It is purely mystical. It is a fantastic dream of a troubled mind. It is probably an allegory; later, Brahmins converted it into a literal statement of hard fact. It does not solve the riddle; on the contrary it creates a riddle—which is why the Brahmins were interested in supporting the theory of *Chaturvarna*.[7]

Thus, from a position of questioning, Ambedkar was very much critical of the status quo of the caste system. To Ambedkar, there is no single origin of caste, it is always plural in number. When Brahmins made themselves as a caste by enclosing themselves, they created the non-Brahmin caste, and subsequently other social groups consolidated as closed social systems. Ambedkar criticises Western scholars' position of linking caste with colour. He says neither colour nor race has anything to do with caste.[8]

Exposing the various defences put forward to support the caste system, Ambedkar has stated that it is not only a division of labour but also division of labourers and that too on the basis of graded inequality. "Caste divides the labourers, caste disassociates work from interest, caste disconnects intelligence from manual labour and caste prevents mobilization."[9]

Ambedkar has also demolished the Arya Samajists' theory of *Chaturvarna*, based on worth and not on birth, as impractical and difficult to achieve. He emphasises the need to reorganise the Hindu society on the principles of Fraternity, Liberty and Equality in order to get away from the evil system of caste.

Analysis of Untouchability

Ambedkar says: "Untouchability is the notion of defilement, pollution, contamination and the ways and means of getting rid of that defilement. It is a case of permanent, hereditary staying which nothing can cleanse."[10] Unlike Gandhi, he firmly believes that untouchability is the product of caste and unless it is destroyed, untouchability will not go. Ambedkar, in his book *The Untouchables: Who Are They?* (1948), dealt in depth with the origin and development of untouchability. The outline of his thesis is that caste Hindus and untouchables do not belong to two different races, but the only difference is that they belong to Tribesmen and Broken Men, respectively, and the Broken Men came to be treated as untouchables. Mohan Larbeer observes that for Ambedkar, race or occupations are not reasons for the origin of untouchability. But contempt and hatred for the Broken Men as for Buddhists by Brahmins and the continuation of beef eating by the Broken Men after it had been given up by others are the two reasons for the origin of untouchability. Untouchables are outside the Varna system and so are called *Avarnas*. According to the understanding of Ambedkar, the Broken Men or Untouchables are those:

- Who lived 'outside' the village, because they were broken due to the tribal war.

- Who came for refuge (to the settled).

- Who did the watch and ward for the settled community.

- Who in return got security and food, which was not shared, and they were not allowed to participate in the life-world of the settled communities.[11]

Ambedkar analysed that caste and untouchability existed even before Manu. Therefore, Manu and Brahmins are not the causes for caste and untouchability, except that they consolidated, codified, canonised and sanctified it.

Having analysed the origin of caste and untouchability, Ambedkar carried on a persistent global campaign against it. In the joint memo presented to the Round Table Conference, the first item was "Equal Citizenship, and Fundamental Rights" declaring the practice of untouchability as illegal. When the Indian Constitution of 1950 was on the way to be unveiled, Ambedkar included abolition of untouchability under Section 17 of Part III related to Fundamental Rights. Ambedkar reacted badly to the identification of Dalits as untouchables by the Hindu social order. The identity as untouchables was imposed on the individual and on the caste by other dominant caste groups, who treated them as agents of pollution. According to Ambedkar, "The real method of breaking up the Caste system was not to bring about inter-caste dinners and inter-caste marriages but to destroy the religious notions on which caste was founded."[12]

Analysis of the Hindu Social Order

The analysis of the Hindu social order with specific reference to the problem of caste and untouchability was of great potential to Ambedkar in providing liberation to Dalits. In analysing Hinduism, he says: "If a Hindu says that he is Hindu because he worships the same God as the Hindu community does, his answer cannot be true. All Hindus do not worship one God. There is no definite creed for Hinduism."[13] Hindus treat Vedas as eternal and infallible, and it is these Vedas that sanctifies the caste system. On Vedas, Ambedkar says, "The Vedas has no authority, since it has the defects of falsehood, self-contradiction and tautology." As to the philosophy: "…there is nothing of it in the Rig-Veda. As Prof. Wilson observes, there is in the Rig-Veda, which is the stock of Veda, scarcely any indication or doctrinal or philosophical speculation, no allusion to the later notions of the several schools, nor is there any hint of metempsychosis, or of the doctrine intimately allied to it, of the repeated renovation of the world. The Vedas may be useful as a source of information regarding the social life of the Aryans. As a picture of primitive life, it is full of curiosity but there is nothing elevating. There are more vices and a few virtues."[14] Thus Ambedkar was very critical of the Vedas, for he says that neither the subject matter nor the contents of the Vedas justify the infallibility with which they have been invested.

Larbeer again observes that for Ambedkar, the Hindu social order is grounded in immorality. It is against justice, liberty, equality and fraternity. It is a cluster of closed units that enclose themselves, leaving no room for relationship and social intercourse. It is an order of self-imprisonment that enslaves the human into caste prisons. It segregates by the 'infection of imitation,' which in turn affects every successive caste group, and ultimately Indian society is caste-ridden. It is a system that degrades and alienates human labour and labourers. It lacks any social conscience for being in union. Spontaneity and moral freedom are alien to the system of the caste social order. Participation and communication for social living is systematically prohibited in it. Its social expression is untouchability or social exclusion whose cumulative effect is laid very heavily on the shoulders of the broken people. Therefore, for Ambedkar, reconstruction of the identity of the broken people and through that the reconstruction of Indian society on a moral basis becomes a life mission.[15] Ambedkar's criticism of the caste social order is inseparable from his criticism of Hindu religion. If he starts with evaluating the caste system, he inevitably ends up with the criticism of the Hindu religion. If he starts with the evaluation of the Hindu religion, he inevitably ends up with the criticism of the caste social order. Thus, Ambedkar analyses the Hindu social order and provides a path towards liberating the untouchables.

Brahminism and Capitalism: The Twin Dangers

Ambedkar held that Indian society is infected with two great dangers. One is internal and the other is external. The internal danger is casteism and the external is capitalism. He says, "The two enemies are Brahminism and Capitalism." By Brahminism he meant the negation of the spirit of liberty, equality and fraternity. In that sense it is rampant in all classes and is not confined to the Brahmins alone though they have been the originators of it. This Brahminism which pervades everywhere and which regulates the thoughts and deeds of all classes is an incontrovertible fact.[16]

Ambedkar was against the monopoly of economy in the hands of the few and straight monopoly. While Brahminism is antagonistic to the liberation of Dalits, capitalism would go to strengthen this process of caste antagonism. He held that the state must play a key role in handling these two dangers and bring about economic equality and political liberty to Dalits. He proposed state socialism and mixed economy as the guarantees of a just economic life for the oppressed sections of Indian society.

Analysis of Religion

Ambedkar gave paramount importance to the issue of religion. Understanding religion, for Ambedkar, is vital to the understanding of the social life of Indian society. For Ambedkar, religion is essential to humankind. He understood religion not as a means to spiritual salvation of individual souls but as a social practice for establishing righteous relations between human and human. He held that religion is the vital force or live wire, a scheme of moral governance and foundation of human society. He regarded religion as necessary for nationalism since religions, as the essence of cultural heritage, have a value system necessary for the formation of a civil and political community and is a necessary factor for building a powerful nation. He criticised Hindu religion, the concept of God and its allied religious principles and customs that tend to preserve the caste system intact. The untouchables were not allowed to get the same status as others in the Hindu religion. Ambedkar believed that absorption of Dalits into Hinduism meant the acceptance of Hindu leadership in the national movement. So he felt it would be wiser to take chances with a religion that has many safeguards. At first, he tried to assert the path of radical autonomy, encouraged Dalits to form their own organisations and to deal independently with some basic issues. It means that Dalits themselves have to redefine their relationship with the Hindu system. In fact, a non-Hindu choice seems to have led him, finally, to identify with Buddhism.[17]

According to Ambedkar, Buddhism was a true religion because it led to a life guided by three principles—knowledge, right path, and compassion. In Buddhism he discovered a ray of hope and light for all communities. Buddhism teaches social freedom, intellectual freedom, economic freedom and political freedom, and equality not between man and man only but also between man and woman. The rational criteria that Ambedkar envisaged for considering a religion to be true and authentic are that it should be based on reason, pass the test of utility and justice and should contain ethical and social content based on the principles of revolution for liberty, equality and fraternity.[18] Thus, Ambedkar analyses religion and says that religion is for humans and not humans for religion.

Directions from Dr. B.R. Ambedkar's Social Analysis to the Church in India

Having discussed Ambedkar's analysis of the socio-religious structures of India, one can draw its relevance in theologising today. The purpose of Ambedkar's analysis is to provide liberation to Dalits. Perhaps, Ambedkar is one who has provided consistent theoretical criticism of the socio-religious structures in India. Ambedkar had a strong background of Western Enlightenment thought that helped him evaluate the Indian social structure from the point of view of liberty, equality and fraternity. The individual and the social are the two complementary vital elements in the theoretical frame of Ambedkar's analysis. As Larbeer puts it, the purpose of Ambedkar's analysis can be classified in two folds. On the one hand Ambedkar wanted to establish the identity of untouchables as an indigenous social religious group that resisted caste inequality from its inception. And on the other, he ignited an ongoing social, educational, political movement, an action for liberation, which would continue to upsurge the cause of justice in Indian society, irrespective of the pains and sufferings in its encounter with the orthodoxy.[19]

What is the relevance of Ambedkar's analysis of the socio-religious structures of India? Gabriele Dietrich and Bas Wielenga in their book *Towards Understanding Indian Society* brings out the need for social analysis. They say:

- We cannot understand people without understanding society.

- We cannot understand society by looking at individuals only.

- We cannot change society purposefully without knowing how we are shaped by it.[20]

They also bring out the need for social analysis in theologising today. Their propositions are:

- We cannot do God's will in social life unless we understand in a critical way how society functions.

- We cannot serve in the ministry of the church without a critical understanding of its role in society.

- All theology is contextual.

- The Bible does not lose but gains in relevance if we analyse how its messages relate to changing social situations.

- We need not just social analysis to clarify the role of faith, but we also need faith to clarify the role of social analysis.[21]

Therefore, Ambedkar's social analysis has a challenging relevance for us today in our theologising. Ambedkar's analysis provides a methodological framework in analysing our own contexts and thereby provides a space for critical faith reflection. The three components of Ambedkar's social analysis are:

1. Equality of opportunity for all citizens.

2. Critique of Hindu society based on liberty, equality and fraternity.

3. Establishment of a casteless society by removing oppression and domination.

Dalit oppression is a continuing reality today in India. Dalits are oppressed, suppressed, marginalised and humiliated in every sphere of life. Today it is the task of the Indian church to participate in the struggles of these people and work towards a liberation of Dalits. Dr. K. Rajaratnam has given a clarion call to the churches in India to make Dalit liberation the agenda of the church. And therefore, it is time for us to analyse Dalit oppression and to critique all the dominant structures of the day as Ambedkar did in his day and liberate our Dalit brothers and sisters. Thus, Ambedkar's social analysis has a challenging relevance to theologise in our times.

Though there are several streams and themes that draw the attention of the church in India, three major themes would be of relevance for the theology of the church's ministries in India.

Proclaim and practice that caste is a sin

The church in India today has been comfortable in making their premises "plastic free." That is a good way of keeping the environment clean and green, and the church needs appreciation for it. I have heard that a certain church in India has proclaimed that using plastics is a sin. But we the church have just remained with that, and think we have used our faith to analyse our society. But when caste system is such a dire reality in India, which is practised even in the church, we the church have not come up to preach, proclaim and practice that "practicing caste is a sin." The time has come now for the churches to rise up to the occasion and boldly proclaim that caste or caste practice is a sin. When we are all created in the equal image of God, how is it that there are caste differences and hierarchy among people? I believe our faith helps us to boldly proclaim that caste is a deadly sin. This is where we need faith to clarify the role of social analysis. Therefore, let us confront and challenge the evil caste system and be bold in doing it. While we have fallen short of God's glory with all our misdeeds, by practising the caste system and oppressing people in the name of caste, I am afraid we are thrown away from the presence of God, for God affirms equality and justice.

Challenge globalisation, a shot in the arm for caste system

Dr. Ambedkar prophetically said that capitalism would strengthen the antagonism of the caste system. It is of great relevance for us to analyse the dangers of globalisation on Indian society and particularly on Dalits and Adivasis. Globalisation has adverse effects on Dalits and Tribals. Without access to technical know-how, Dalits and Tribals are nowhere in the arena of globalisation. Globalisation promotes consumerism and profit values and does not value life and life-centred values. Globalisation preaches and proclaims hierarchy and widens the gap between the rich and the poor, the haves and the have-nots. Therefore, for the practitioners of caste in India, globalisation has come as a shot in the arm, for they can use it to further suppress and marginalise Dalits and Tribals. Globalisation does not care who is the loser, whether it is a Dalit or a Tribal; all it wants and gets is profit, and that is exactly what the caste system likes and expects. So, the caste system utilises this chance of globalisation and uses it to further suppress Dalits and Tribals.

When such a situation exists in our society, how can we the church in India slumber? We the church should analyse the situation, and should come out with a preferential option for Dalits and Tribals in India. Confront caste system and globalisation, for they are the twin dangers in our society today. If justice is to roll down in our society, we the church should be just and should analyse society justly, with a concern and preference for Dalits and Tribals.

Conversion 'from' vis-à-vis conversion 'to'

Time and again we the church in India have discussed the importance of conversion, and particularly conversion of Dalits. Conversion for Dr. Ambedkar was necessary because it was a means of liberation, for he did not want to endorse the status quo of the caste system practised by a particular religion. Dr. Ambedkar's words of "I am born as a Hindu, but do not want to die as a Hindu" has been misinterpreted by evangelists today that his words endorse conversion, a call for us to convert people to Christianity. Dr. K. Rajaratnam has already observed that 'conversion from' is of prime importance for Dalits rather than 'conversion to'; and let Dalits take their own decision in terms of choosing their religion. Let us not take Dalits for a ride, take them for granted and resort to forced conversions. In this context, I believe we the church should be in solidarity with the attempts of Dalits when they prefer conversion as a means of liberation. In following the words of Jesus Christ, "Setting at liberty all that are oppressed," we the church should strive and help Dalits to overcome their oppression and stand by them in their struggles. We the church should work for Dalits and start implementing the agenda of the church in our local contexts.

Conclusion

Dr. B.R. Ambedkar was a great social revolutionary and thinker of modern India. He minutely observed the fallacies of social, economic and political structures of Indian society, the ideological overtone that justified and supported them and paved the path for graded inequality and perpetual exploitation and suppression of the have-nots. Ambedkar vehemently opposed and fought against them throughout his life. He remains immortal by his deeds. He was very firm in telling that there should be a political partition between the untouchables and the Hindus. He rejected the Brahminical dominance, paving the way for liberation and has become the champion of Dalits. Dr. Ambedkar's socio-religious analysis has great relevance in analysing our own societies today, and let the church be sensitive in analysing its local contexts and start living up to the values of the gospel. We as a church should confront the evils of society, preach and practice that caste is sin, confront globalisation and be in solidarity with Dalits in their efforts for liberation. Let the church in India draw inspiration from the work of Dr. Ambedkar in liberating all who are oppressed, particularly Dalits. Let us unitedly and univocally cast out caste.

Endnotes

[1] Vasant Moon (Ed.) *Dr. Babasaheb Ambedkar: Writings and Speeches. Vol.4.* (Bombay: Govt. of Maharashtra, 1987), 1

[2] Sanjay Paswan & Paramanshi Jaideva (Eds). *Encyclopedia of Dalits in India. Vol.I*, (Delhi: Kalpaz Publications, 2002), 221.

[3] Gail Omvedt, *Dalits and The Democratic Revolution*, (Delhi: Sage, 1994), 91.

[4] Vidhu Varma, "Colonialism and Liberation, Ambedkar's Quest for Distributive Justice," in *Economic & Political Weekly*, Sept.25, 1999, 2805.

[5] D.K. Baisantry, *Ambedkar: The Total Revolutionary*, (New Delhi: Segment book, 1991), 78.

[6] Vasant Moon (Ed.) *Dr. Babasaheb Ambedkar: Writings and Speeches*, *Vol.4.* (Bombay: Govt. of Maharashtra, 1987), 203-204.

[7] Vasant Moon (Ed), 251

[8] P. Mohan Larbeer, *Ambedkar on Religion*, (New Delhi: ISPCK, 2003), 25-26.

[9] R. Sangeetha Rao, *Ambedkar on Varna, Caste and Class*, (New Delhi: Sanjivayya Institute of Socio-Economic Studies), 10.

[10] P. Mohan Larbeer, 27.

[11] P. Mohan Larbeer, 37.

[12] Vasant Moon (Ed), Vol.1, 21.

[13] Vasant Moon (Ed), Vol.4, 13-14.

[14] Vasant Moon (Ed), Vol.4, 44.

[15] P. Mohan Larbeer, 157.

[16] P. Mohan Larbeer, 71.

[17] Vidhu Varma, "Colonialism and Liberation, Ambedkar's Quest for Distributive Justice," in *Economic & Political Weekly*, Sept. 25, 1999, 2805.

[18] P. Mohan Larbeer, 185.

[19] P. Mohan Larbeer, 159.

[20] Gabriele Dietrich and Bas Wielenga. *Towards Understanding Indian Society*, (Tiruvalla: CSS, 2003), 17-19

[21] Ibid., 20-22.

Chapter - 4

Pain, Pathos and *Peta:*
A.P. Nirmal's Dalit Theology

Introduction

Dalit theology, as an Indian liberation theology, has a come a long way since it made inroads into Indian Christian theology by the articulations of A.P. Nirmal in 1981. Taking cognisance of Dalit realities in the Indian church and the Indian public, Dalit theology emerged as a counter-theology, countering the dominant publics of casteism. It has also been a protest theology against the forces of marginalisation, domination and oppression. For the last three and a half decades, Dalit theology has been growing in its influence, impact and relevance and has been appealing to the contexts of the Indian public sphere.

Dalit theology emerged as a counter-public theology, countering the theological hierarchy Indian Christian theology has been enjoying for so long. As M.E. Prabhakar says, "Dalit theology emerged as a counter-theological movement, seeking to construct 'an authentically Indian Liberation theology' on behalf of Dalits."[1] Therefore, one has to understand that Dalit theology evolved out of a theological and a contextual necessity in countering the public sphere, which are defined by the parameters—the Indian Christian theological academia, the Indian church and the Indian society.

In this chapter I want to present to you discussions on Dalit theology from the contributions of A.P. Nirmal, who has been the pioneer of Dalit theology in India. Nirmal boldly made theological propositions towards Dalit theology as a counter-theology, and having come from a Dalit locality, *peta,* he had a passion for the liberation of Dalits. His theological articulation was based on the plight and pathos of Dalits.

This chapter is an attempt to bring into light Nirmal's Dalit Theology, its methodology and other ingredients in his theology.

Etymology of the word 'Dalit'

According to A.P. Nirmal, Dalit theology is concerned with a people who are denied their essential humanhood. He also says that Dalits are the "no people" of the New Testament. In terms of the Varna system of Hindu society, they are *Avarnas*—outside the fourfold caste structure. The term 'Dalit' means 1) the broken, the torn, the rent, the burst, the split; 2) the opened, the expended; 3) the bisected; 4) the driven asunder, the dispelled, the scattered; 5) the downtrodden, the crushed, the destroyed; 6) the manifested, the displayed.[2]

Basic Theme of Dalit Literature

Nirmal says: "It goes without saying that the most basic theme of Dalit literature in Marathi is 'total human liberation.' The theme is derived from the unshakable faith in human dignity and the inviolability of the human spirit. The basic theme is developed within the framework of oppression of Dalits. Dalit literature is a protest on behalf of self-determination and for an end to social and religious subjugation. The protest is deeply rooted in the pathos of Dalit life. For centuries, Dalits have lived a miserable subhuman life. Dalit autobiographies describe the miseries of Dalits in the past and also the present. Dr. B.R. Ambedkar is the hero of Dalit literature." Therefore, according to Nirmal, Christian Dalit theology has much to learn from Dalit literature. Dalit literature serves as a mirror that reflects the past, the present and the future of Christian Dalits in India.[3]

Why Dalit Theology?

Nirmal traces the tradition of Indian Christian theology and feels the need for an extension for Indian Christian theology. Thus far Indian theologians have ignored the reality of the Indian church. As many as 50-80 per cent of Christians in India are of Scheduled Caste origin. Nirmal therefore feels that there is an urgent need for Dalit theology. The need for a Dalit theology emerged as a critique of classical Indian theology, Liberation theology and Ecumenical theology in India.

Critique of Classical Indian Christian Theology

Nirmal says, "Indian Christian Theology (ICT) in the past has tried to work out its theological systems in terms of either Advaita Vedanta or Vaishisahtha Advaita. Most of the contributions to ICT in the past came from caste converts to Christianity. The result has been that ICT has perpetuated within itself what I prefer to call the 'Brahminic' tradition (Bishop A.J. Appasamy's *Bhakti Marga*, Brahma Bandhav Upadhyaya's synthesis of Advaita and Christian theology, M.M. Thomas's theological anthropology in *Karma Marga* and Chenchiah's synthesis of Christian theology with Aurobindo's *Integral Yoga*). This tradition has further perpetuated intuition-interiority oriented approach to the theological task in India. One wonders whether this kind of Christian theology will ever have a mass appeal."[4] Thus Nirmal feels the need for Dalit theology, which will be relevant and contextual.

Critique of Indian Ecumenical Theology

India has a rich tradition and legacy in the world ecumenical movement, and it has stood as one of the pioneers in laying down the foundations of the modern ecumenical movement. Nirmal says that from the early days of India's ecumenical involvement, it has concerned itself with the problem of other faiths. Out of this ecumenical involvement emerged the concern for dialogue with other living faiths, and this concern continuous to be taken seriously. But Nirmal says that this concern has contributed to ICT's obsession with the Brahminic tradition.[5]

Critique of Liberation Theology

Nirmal feels that Liberation theology, which was born and baptised in Latin America, is yet another imported theology. Though the liberation motif has its relevance for the poor in India, Nirmal feels that liberation motifs in India are of a different nature. The Latin American Liberation theology used Marxist analysis of socio-economic realities, and such an analysis is inadequate in India. It neglects the caste factor, which adds to the complexity of Indian socio-economic realities. The Indian advocates of Third World theology ignored the incidents of violence against Dalits.[6]

Nirmal also says that somehow our Indian theologies failed to see Dalit movements and struggles as having a potential for theological reflection. Therefore, Nirmal argues that there is a strong need for a Dalit theology which appeals to the masses.

What is Dalit Theology?

Nirmal says this question may be answered in at least three different ways:

1. The first answer may be that it is a theology about Dalits or theological reflection upon the Christian responsibility to the depressed classes.

2. The answer may be that it is a theology for the depressed classes or the theology of the message addressed to the depressed classes and to which they seem to be responding.

3. The answer may be that it is a theology from the depressed classes, that is the theology which they themselves would like to expound.[7]

Christian Dalit theology, according to Nirmal, will be a counter-theology. When asked what is Christian in Dalit theology, Nirmal says it is the *Dalitness* which is 'Christian' about Dalit theology. The 'Christian' for this theology is exclusively the 'Dalit'. It is the common Dalit experience of Christian Dalits along with other Dalits that will shape a Dalit Christian theology. It is therefore a people's theology.

Methodology of Dalit Theology

Since Dalit theology is a people's theology, the primary datum for doing this theology is people. The word "people" here becomes a theological category, a theological concept. It is both a theological concept and a sociological reality.

Dalit Theology and Sociology

Because Dalits are a sociological reality, Dalit theology has social and sociological dimensions. Classical theological tradition regarded philosophy as the most adequate medium for communicating Christian theological truths. Indian Christian theology is not an exception. According to Nirmal, for liberation theologies, including Dalit theology, social realities are more important than philosophical prepositional consistencies. This change in stance also implies a social and sociological critique of classical theologies. There is a movement from philosophy to sociology. One of the methodological implications is that Dalit theology serves the Dalit people by empowering them for their liberation struggle. Another implication is that Dalit theology is from below and is more interested in the horizontal relations than in the vertical revelation.[8]

Pathos as the basis of Dalit Theology

Liberation theologies in general have rejected the priority of theory and thought. They have affirmed the basic unity between theory and practice, and thought and action. They have affirmed that all knowing is praxiological. While Dalit theology, because of its liberation motifs, will not question this praxiological basis of human knowledge, it would want to affirm that pathos is prior to praxis. Dalit theology wants to assert that at the heart of the Dalit people's experience is pathos or suffering. This pathos or suffering or pain is prior to their involvement in any activist struggle for liberation. For a Dalit theology, "Pain or Pathos is the beginning of knowledge." For the sufferer, more certain than any principle, more certain than any proposition, more certain than any thought and more certain than any action, is his/her pain-pathos. It is in and through this pain-pathos that the sufferer knows God. This is because the sufferer in and through his/her pain-pathos knows that God participates in human pain.

Nirmal says that many people have asked him if he has ruled out the possibility of Dalit theology done by non-Dalits. The answer to such a question must be a complex one. Nirmal says, "I would maintain that there are three different modes of knowing. These are the pathetic knowing, the empathetic knowing and the sympathetic knowing." At the heart of this pathos epistemology is Nirmal's understanding of the incarnation. If God wants to participate in human pain then He/She must become human. Non-Dalits can at best "empathize" with the Dalit cause. But the 'pathetic' knowing is the prerogative of Dalits themselves. Dalit theology thus can be attempted at different levels. But authentic Dalit theology must arise out of Dalit pain-pathos.[9]

Methodological Exclusivism

Dalit theology must observe a methodological exclusivism in relation to other theologies. A methodological exclusivism does not imply a community exclusivism. As a community, Dalits must be open to other communities and other peoples. They must also promote all horizontal community relationships. But methodological exclusivism is a different matter. Dalit theology is a counter-theology. The tendency of all dominant theological traditions is to accommodate, include, assimilate and finally conquer other theologies. If Dalit theology has to play the role of a counter-theology, then it must adopt an exclusivist stance and shut off the encroaching influences of the dominant theologies. Nirmal says this methodological exclusivism is necessary for maintaining the distinctive identity of Dalit theology.[10]

Dalit Theology—A theology of identity

The question of the distinctive identity of this theology is inseparably linked with the identity of the Dalit people. All people's theologies are really theologies of identity. The dominant theological traditions are invariably intolerant of theology and cultural pluralism and they suppress the identities of the oppressed people. People's theologies then seek to express the distinctive identities of their respective people. A search and expression of identity therefore characterises all liberative theologies and people's theologies. The question of identity is the question of the concerned people's roots and their historical consciousness.

History is important for them, but the current dominant historiographer is not on their side. More often than not the Dalit people have no written historical traditions. Their histories are oral histories based on oral traditions. What is really needed is historical scholarship that is "interested" in Dalit issues and which will look at oral traditions more sympathetically and consider them as "alternative" historical sources. Such scholarship may have to start with the "family histories" of Dalits. Apart from oral traditions, it is also necessary that the rituals, rites and festivals of Dalits are studied with a view to understanding their distinctive history and culture. Dalit histories thus are important for doing Dalit theologies. But such past-oriented history alone will not be sufficient for doing Dalit theology. Dalit theology must also be informed by a social vision, which is liberative in character.[11]

Towards Dalit Hermeneutics

Nirmal exegetes the Deuteronomic creed in Deuteronomy 26:5-12 as having tremendous implications for Dalit theology. He draws out five important implications for Dalit theology from this passage.

1.   "A wandering Aramean was my father," recalls the nomadic consciousness. To confess that 'once we were no people' is also an integral part of a confession before we come to the claim that now we are God's people.

2.   "Few in number" represents the entire community. In our search for a Dalit theology, it is well worth remembering that what we are looking for is community-identity, community-roots and community-consciousness.

3.   "The suffering and bondage in Egypt." A Christian Dalit theology, therefore, is a story of the afflictions, the bondage, the harsh treatment, the toil and the tears of Dalits.

4.   "The Exodus liberation is symbolised by a mighty hand, terror, signs and wonders." Dalits must protest and agitate to change their life.

5.   "Land flowing with milk and honey." It is an outcome of the liberation already achieved. Liberation is its own reward.

This historical Deuteronomic creed has a paradigmatic value for our Dalit theological construct. The Dalit consciousness should realise that the ultimate goal of its liberation moment is the realisation of our full humanness, or conversely, our full divinity, the ideal of the image of God in us.[12] Nirmal tries to attempt a reader-response hermeneutics in his Dalit theology. The historical consciousness of the plight of Dalits has primacy over the historical critical methods.

Dalit God

According to Nirmal, a non-Dalit deity cannot be the God of Dalits. So, the God whom Jesus Christ revealed is a Dalit God. He is a servant God—a God who serves. Service of others has always been the privilege of Dalit communities. The amazing claim of a Christian Dalit theology, according to Nirmal, will be that their God, the self-existent, the *svayambhoo,* does not create others to do servile work, but does servile work himself.

Servitude is innate in the God of Dalits. Nirmal says that our God is a servant God. He is a waiter, a dhobi, a bhangi. To speak of a servant God, therefore, is to recognise and identify him as a truly Dalit deity.[13] Dalit God is well represented in the servant-song of Isaiah as mentioned in chapter 53.

Dalit Christology

Being Christian Dalits has a Christological implication, according to Nirmal. It means we are the followers of Jesus Christ who himself was a Dalit. Both his humanity and his divinity are to be understood in terms of Dalitness.

1.   In the genealogy of Jesus, a few of his ancestors like Tamar, Rahab and Bethsheba reveal the illegitimacy of Jesus, and this is suggestive of his Dalit condition. Even the expression 'a carpenter's son' also hints at his Dalitness.

2.   The title that Jesus preferred to use for himself is 'the Son of Man.' It is used to mean a simple man, indicative of Jesus' sufferings and imminent death. Mark 8:31, 9:12, 10:45 reveal that Jesus underwent Dalit experiences, like rejection, mockery, contempt, etc., as the prototype of all Dalits.

3.   Jesus' total identification with the Dalits of his day like the publicans, tax collectors, Samaritans and sinners manifests his Dalitness.

4.   The Nazareth Manifesto as mentioned in Luke 4:16-19 is really a manifesto for Dalits This also reveals the Dalitness of Jesus.

5.   Jesus' Dalitness is best symbolised by the cross, for he was broken, crushed, split, torn on it. And as Son of God, his

feeling that he is forsaken by God also reveals the Dalitness of his divinity.[14]

Dalit Pneumatology

According to Nirmal, the Holy Spirit is the *comforter* for Dalit sufferings and afflictions. The Holy Spirit is the one who revives the dry bones in Ezekiel 37 as much as the Dalits and unifies them into an army. While Peter was preaching, the Holy Spirit descended even on the Gentiles. The Holy Spirit did not wait for the baptism of the Gentiles—the Dalits—to descend upon them. The Holy Spirit is the Spirit on the side of the Dalits.[15]

Ambedkar and Dalit Theology

The writings and speeches of Babasaheb Ambedkar are an inexhaustible source for expounding his multifaceted thought. Nirmal says, "We should note the point that any version of Christian Dalit theology has to come to grips with Ambedkar's thinking and face its challenges and appropriate its insights. We believe that any attempts at Dalit theology will have to pay attention to the Dalit reality as a whole—with its historical, cultural, social, economic, political and artistic aspects. That is where Babasaheb's significance lies. He looked at the Dalit question from different angles but in an inter-disciplinary and inter-related way."[16] Thus Nirmal brings out the relevance of Ambedkar for Dalit theology.

Conclusion

Dalit theology has come long way since April 1981 when A.P. Nirmal attempted to construct a Dalit theology. It is for sure that Nirmal's Dalit theology has opened up several new avenues in the Dalit theological arena, and a series of attempts and initiatives have succeeded him in systematically articulating

Christian faith in the context of the newly emerging Dalit aspiration for liberation.

Nirmal's Dalit theology deserves commendation, specially for the way he theologised from within the Christian faith. For Dalits, what is in front of the text is more important rather than what is behind the text, and Nirmal's hermeneutics of reader-response deserve appreciation. On the other hand, Nirmal's methodological exclusivism for Dalit theology has had to receive some criticism. Today, knowledge is not like a pyramid, but rather as, Imre Lakatose says, knowledge is like a 'network.' And if at all Dalit theology needs to hold on in academic circles, I think it has to open itself to other voices and sciences so that it becomes rich in its content and newer in its dimensions. So, I think, time has come for us to move ahead of Nirmal in this methodological exclusivism of Dalit theology. Nirmal was always concerned about Christian Dalits, and has nothing to say about non-Christian Dalits or Dalits *per se*. Is Nirmal comfortable when today other theologians say that liberation 'from' is more important than liberation 'to'? Nirmal is silent on the theology of the liberation of the oppressor. Is there a space in his theology for the liberation of the oppressor?

Nirmal, being the pioneer in Dalit theology, responded more to his context, and his creative contributions made a mark and added new strength to the theological enterprise in India. Nirmal's Dalit theology is a theology of hope, directing Dalits to seek liberation through the God of the oppressed. His theology gave the Indian church a new awareness of its own identity and provided a new direction in its mission to liberate the oppressed.

Endnotes

[1] M.E. Prabhakar "The Search for a Dalit Theology," in James Massey, ed. *Indigenous People: Dalit Issues in Today's Theological Debate*, (Delhi: ISPCK, 1994), 213.

[2] A.P. Nirmal, "What is Dalit Theology," *NCC Review* 108/2 (February 1988), 71.

[3] A.P. Nirmal, "A Dialogue with Dalit Literature," in *Towards a Dalit Theology*, edited by M.E. Prabhakar (Delhi: ISPCK, 1988), 73-75.

[4] A.P. Nirmal, *Heuristic Explorations*, (Madras: CLS, 1990), 139.

[5] A.P. Nirmal, "What is Dalit Theology," 73.

[6] *Ibid*, 73-74.

[7] *Ibid*, 75-76.

[8] A.P. Nirmal, "Doing Theology from a Dalit Perspective," in *Voices from the Third World* 16/2 (December, 1993), 170-171.

[9] Ibid, 171-173.

[10] Ibid, 173-174.

[11] Ibid, 174-175.

[12] A.P. Nirmal, "What is Dalit Theology," 77-80

[13] Ibid, 81-83.

[14] Ibid, 83-85.

[15] Ibid, 85-86.

[16] A.P. Nirmal, "Introduction," in *Dr. B.R. Ambedkar: A Centenary Tribute*, edited by A.P. Nirmal and V. Devasahayam (Madras: GLTCRI, 1991), i.

Part II

The Locus of *Dalitekklesia:* Perspectives

This part discusses the perspectives
in the understanding of a church from below

Chapter 5

Multiple Identities of Dalit Christians: Perspectives & Possibilities

Introduction

Dalit Christians' identity has been layered into several strands in today's sociopolitical and religious India. The social identity of Dalits of any religion, for that matter, is critical. From the perspective of other castes, Dalits continue to be Dalits no matter which religion they adhere to. So their caste identity does not change with conversion. Dalit Christians, who gets converted to Christianity, face several challenges in their journey towards liberation. In the discussions on the identity of Dalit Christians, there is a challenge and prospect arising out of their multiple identities. This discussion on the multiple identities of Dalit Christians becomes important, with the rise in numbers of Dalit Christians in the churches of India today. In order to help us understand the issue of Dalit identity, I begin with a case study.

The Case Study on Dalit Christian Identity

Joshua Peter, a Christian from Scheduled Caste (Mala) origin in Andhra Pradesh takes his daughter Mary to get her admitted in the local panchayat school, taking a day off from his routine agricultural labour, which he does for his livelihood. The upper caste Hindu teacher in the school briefs Joshua to enrol his daughter Mary with another name so that she can avail scholarships, mid-day meal facilities and other benefits under the Scheduled Caste status granted by the government, for a Christian name and identity may not guarantee such facilities. Thus, Joshua had to think of another name, which may be Hindu or non-denominational, but not overtly Christian. With the consent of her father, the teacher enrols Mary as Raja Kumari, and the child is forced to remember her new name for the sake of attendance. Joshua's dismal economic condition forces him to declare them officially as Hindu (Adi Andhra Mala) to qualify for SC benefits; however, they continue to practice Christianity in their day-to-day life, associating with the life of the Church. The official identity of the Dalit Christians in Andhra Pradesh, which is a Hindu one, is only a declared identity, not a professed or practiced one.[1]

This narrative provides the perspective in the formation of identity for Dalit Christians, right from their childhood, to practice and get used to their Hindu name in 'public' and to hold on to their Christian faith in 'private.' Forcing on a new identity onto little Mary has several repercussions on her self-identity, self-belief and self-dignity. Mary has a Christian identity by faith, a Hindu identity by law and continues with her outcaste identity by experience, having been born into a Dalit Mala family.

Christians of the Scheduled Caste origin, popularly known as Dalit Christians in India today, form 1.3 per cent of the total population and about 80 per cent of the Indian Christian population which experiences discrimination and exclusion in every quarter of life. A Dalit Christian like Mary, also called Raja Kumari, continues to undergo alienation, humiliation and marginalisation and suffers from a fivefold discrimination: i) from the hostile Hindu society, for she is from an untouchable community, ii) from the unfriendly government since she affirms her faith in Christianity as Dalit, iii) from fellow Hindu Dalits for availing the benefits of the Scheduled Caste though she does not practice Hindu faith, iv) from the unredeemed caste-minded Christian community, who thinks Mary and her family are lower to them in caste, and v) from the sub-groups of Dalit Christians themselves, who think they are the chosen ones and who have sacrificed their benefits for the faith while Mary is unfaithful to the commitment of Christian faith for subscribing to be legally Hindu.

Added to these discriminations, the identity of Dalit Christians has been at risk for there are multiple identities that are imposed on them and they are further pushed to marginality. On the other hand, the identity is a symbol of resilience. There has always been a dialectical tension between the two trajectories of identities for Dalit Christians, which provide a challenge and prospect. To understand this, it would be worth knowing how the category of Dalit Christians emerged or evolved.

Dalits' Conversion to Christianity

The history of Christianity in India has enough records on 'mass conversions' among Dalits. The largest number of Dalits that converted to Christianity was in Andhra Pradesh when John Clough, the Baptist missionary, led these conversions. There have been several debates around these 'mass conversions.' What caused such huge conversions? Were they allured to convert? Were they converted for material benefits? Were the conversions for purposes of mobility from oppression? The questions continue, however to understand conversions of Dalits to Christianity, I would put forth two worldviews on conversions from history, one from Gandhi and the other from Ambedkar.

Conversion for Convenience

Gandhi has been a strong critic of Christian missions and religious conversions, for he has always emphasised spiritual motives *vis-à-vis* material motives. Gandhi even labelled conversion as "the deadliest poison that ever sapped the fountain of truth." As a proponent of *swadeshi*, Gandhi found conversion to Christianity objectionable because he claimed that conversion discounted the great truths in the Indian tradition, and it also amounted to 'denationalisation.' He also believed that conversion of Dalits to Christianity was merely a matter of 'convenience,' motivated by the need to fill their stomachs than a spiritual transformation. He even likened preaching the gospel to a Dalit to preaching it to a cow.[2]

This was a view that influenced most critics of Christian missions and the adherents of Hindutva, including Arun Shourie recently. Most of those belonging to this school of thought assume that Dalits are like dumb cows, who do not apply their mind or intellect when considering conversion to other faiths, and that they choose the material benefits given by Christian mission organisations. This drives Dalits in general, and Dalit Christians in particular, further to the margins, for in their vulnerability, conversions have further added salt to the wounds of Dalits.

Conversion as Autonomy

Ambedkar represents the other school of thought. He affirms conversions for Dalits as a fight for separation and autonomy from Hindu religion and society. He was also critical of Gandhi's view on conversion, for Gandhi's double standards were applied to Muslims and Christians. Ambedkar also was critical of Gandhi's proposition that all religions are equal. Ambedkar pointed out that it is precisely because all religions are not equal that Dalits choose to go for other religions that affirm equality to them. Conversion, Ambedkar opined, "is as important to the Untouchable as self-government is to India."[3]

This school of thought, whom Ambedkar represents, believes that conversion paves the way for mobility from the cruel discriminatory caste for liberation and transformation. Dalits, in this case, chose to convert to Christianity to affirm a life of dignity, which was not provided in their previous religions. Christianity provided a way of life, a sense of equality and a spirituality of combat and resistance in fighting against the forces of discrimination.

Dalit hyphenated Christian

As Dalits convert to Christianity, many Christian leaders have maintained that 'there is no longer male or female, master or slave, Jew or gentile…' and therefore no longer do they exist as Dalits, but as full Christians. But in reality, despite the conversion of religion, there is no conversion of caste, for the baggage of caste identity continues within and outside the church. Is Dalit an adjective to the Christian identity for Dalit Christians, qualifying the Christian-ness or is it vice versa? Is Dalit Christian a noun by itself? More than a debate on the 'parts of speech,' it is the Dalit-ness that qualifies the Christian-ness and the Christian-ness that qualifies the Dalit-ness in the Dalit Christian identity. Consciousness is a key to Dalit identity, however different this consciousness may be. It needs to be acknowledged that there is diversity in the Dalit-Christian perception of this identity. This ranges from identifying oneself as solely Christian, one who has relinquished one's Dalit past, to identifying oneself as solely

Dalit, one who is yet to be active in the church. Between these two are several who consciously alternate between Dalit secular identity and religious Christian identity, with multiple layers of consciousness. Multiple liabilities suffered by Dalit Christians in terms of discrimination, according to John Webster, gave rise to a distinct Dalit consciousness even within the Christian circles.[4]

The Dialectical Tensions between Dalit and Christian Identity

Several studies have shown the tension between the 'continuity-discontinuity' from the Dalit cultures to the Christian ethos that Dalit Christians encounter as Dalits convert to Christianity. In the 'conversion-reversion' of Dalit Christians, Harper proposes, "converts move back and forth between old ritual and caste practices and the new Christian identity." According to Harper, "Bishop V.S. Azariah presented Anglican Christianity to Andhra's depressed classes as a dramatic alternative to their former religious practices and was often frustrated by the tendency of converts to treat the new faith and its practices as complements to the old."[5]

M.E. Prabhakar further described this movement between the old Dalit rituals and the new Christian appropriations as 'dialectical existentialism,' a term used to refer to the two-dimensional consciousness among Dalit Christians. As these dialectical tensions brooded over Dalit Christian identities, the exclusions and discrimination that they encountered continued to challenge and shape Christian consciousness among Dalit Christians.

By faith Christian, by law Hindu, by experience Outcaste: Dalit Christian's Multiple Layers of Identity

Every Dalit Christian, after conversion, is a sum total of several identities. This is the case especially because of the discrimination and exclusion of Christians of Scheduled Caste origin by the Indian state over the past 61 years. By not ascribing the Scheduled Caste (SC) status on Dalit Christians, it has brought to the fore several challenges to the identity of Dalit Christians. The 1950 Presidential Order of the Indian Constitution deprives justice and equal rights to Dalits who were converted to Christianity and Islam and denies them the Scheduled Caste status, unlike other Dalit brothers and sisters who were converted to Hinduism, Buddhism and Sikhism.

In this context, Christians of Scheduled Caste origin, despite their loyalty to their Christian faith, have registered themselves as Hindus in their caste certificates in order to avail themselves of the benefits given by the government, such as educational scholarships, opportunities to contest in legislative elections in reserved constituencies and security under the Scheduled Castes and Scheduled Tribes (Prevention of Atrocities) Act, commonly known as the Prevention of Atrocities Act (POA). This multiple identity is something unique to Dalit Christians alone, for their counterparts like Dalit Hindus, Dalit Sikhs and Dalit Buddhists all enjoy both the constitutional rights of the Scheduled Castes and the freedom of religion by openly professing and practising their own faith in this land of secularism.

Ashok Kumar and Rowena Robinson explain the dual identity (Hindu & Christian) among Dalit Christians "as a symbol of the group's sub-ordination/marginality and also a product of structurally imposed marginality. As a product, dual identity emerges as the outcome of the need to cope with concerns about identity and social marginality."[6] This calls for a discussion on this multiple identity within Dalit Christians, considered as both a challenge and as a prospect; it is a challenge in terms of the imposed marginality and struggle that these Dalit Christians undergo, and a prospect in terms of expressing their resilience to the continuing exclusion and discrimination that they undergo.

Multiple Identities and Multiplicity of Marginality

It was not a voluntary choice for Joshua Peter to enrol Mary as a Hindu in her school, but since his context demanded it, he had to succumb to the state's political ploy of forcing its citizens to be under the rubric of Hinduism. With these multiple identities, Mary, who for the purpose of records is called Raja Kumari, continues to undergo severe humiliation from her peers, in her community and in her church as well, which is not an exception from discrimination. Little Mary undergoes the challenge of holding together her multiple identities intact and in that process faces a mutilating and multiplicity of marginality in her life and in her identity. For want of time, allow me to present the marginality from three quarters that impact the Dalit Christian, Mary.

Marginality from Church

The church, which objectively needs to be a place of equality and which believes in justice for all human beings, unfortunately has fallen into the trap of allowing caste prejudices to overtake and overrule. Mary and her family are discriminated in the church, for they are looked down upon as weak people who could not live up to the faith in Jesus Christ and as those who have compromised their faith in the testing furnace the Indian state provides by denying them the SC status.

Mary and her family are denied the rituals and sacraments that the church gives to other Christians of a homogeneous identity, Christian both by law and by practice. Mary and her family members are denied membership in the church, and thereby denied participation in the governance of the church. Mary and her family members, who have multiple identities, would not be allowed to marry other mono-identity Christians, for they think of their superiority and purity over these Dalit Christians. The church brands these Dalit Christians with multiple identities as unchristian and unspiritual. Therefore, these Dalit Christians are further pushed to the margins of the church, facing further discrimination and exclusion.

Marginality from Community

The school in which Mary attends is the first social space during which these multiple identities are solidified in her. Identity formation takes places here in this space. The upper caste Hindu teacher who urged Mary's father to enrol her as a Hindu looks down upon Mary and discriminates against her in school, for Mary will not be treated as equal to the other Hindus in her class. In educational institutions, SC Dalit Christians are marginalised and humiliated since upper caste students think reservation is a shortcut to such places and merit is discounted. The community, which is casteist in its outlook, looks down upon Dalit Christians, for they say these Dalit Christians receive benefits both from the church and from the Indian state because they are legally Hindu Dalits. This, in reality, is not true, for the church discriminates against these Dalit Christians. Therefore, these Dalit Christians with multiple identities are vulnerable and are condemned to marginality both from the church and the community in which they live.

Marginality within Self-identity

With marginality coming from both social spaces, the church and society, Mary struggles within herself to hold together her multiple identities. There is a trauma within her as to who she is, in terms of her identity—a Christian by faith, a Hindu by law and an outcaste by experience. The society pushes Mary and her family further into marginality and they are made to feel guilty for though they are Christian, they are really not, and though they are Hindu, they are really not and their exclusion within the church and society knows no bounds. Identity is formed in freedom, and given the context of marginality, their self-identity is at risk, for it demoralises one's self-worth.

Condemned to marginality thus, Dalit Christians, rather than realising their self-identity, are left to live with these multiple identities that do not help them affirm life and identity in all its fullest sense. These multiple identities multiply the marginality of Dalit Christians and shrink the social space in which they can affirm who they are. The psyche of Dalit Christians is further wounded to its core with all these multiple identities around them. Multiple identities for Dalit Christians have been a challenge, and the stress on them to cope with these identities and live a life of justice is high.

Multiple Identities as Symbol of Resilience for Dalit Christians

On the other hand, despite associating marginality with their identity, for Dalit Christians these multiple identities serve as a symbol of resilience in overcoming their experiences of pollution and marginality that they have been undergoing.

On observing the faith of Dalit Christians in eastern India, R.S. Khare says: "The non-Christian wider society calls the

Christians 'Chamar Christians,' but they are 'Dalit Christians.' 'Chamar' is a received, inherited identity. They have attached the 'Dalit' prefix as part of the new consciousness. The Christian dimension of the identity expressed itself earlier as 'Chamar Christians' or 'Harijan Christians.' At the time, legally and politically they were referred to as the Depressed Classes. These terms have been replaced with 'Dalit Christians' and 'Scheduled Caste Christians' respectively. Their Christian identity seems to represent their symbolic and religious re-formulation; a break from their past; their attempt to assume greater equality, freedom and justice and to seek a new worldview under an alternate socio-religious system. Opting for this system is a 'repossession' of personal and social capabilities and a 'calculated cultural move' towards attained desired aims."[7]

Multiple Identities as Affirming the Mobility to Equality

On receiving multiple identities, Dalit Christians affirm their mobility towards equality; for by asserting their identities, these Dalit Christians have a space to transfer their consciousness from oppression to liberation, from forces of death to life. Multiple identities are an expression of hope towards a new life, for once they were fully crushed under the rubric of caste, but a religious conversion has given them a new identity, and a new life, despite their caste remaining the same. Dr. B.R. Ambedkar tried for special electorates for Dalits as a way out to affirm equality with others, but when it did not come true in history, he called for religious conversion as a way out. So, in 1935, the year when Gandhi made the controversial statement—"If I had power and could legislate, the first thing I would ban is conversions"—Ambedkar also made a historical statement on religious conversions—"Though I have been born a Hindu, I shall not die as a Hindu."[8]

Therefore, with religious conversions of Dalits to Christianity, multiple identities evolved and that led them to a life of self-respect and self-dignity. Mary and her family, particularly her father Joshua Peter, who has been a victim of caste for generations, bore the brunt of discrimination within the caste system. Conversion to Christianity was autonomy for him and his family in running away from the forces of caste. And on becoming Dalit Christian, his multiple identities helped him towards discontinuity from his old culture of being oppressed and towards a life of liberation.

Multiple Identities as a way of Expressing Resilience

Dalit Christians with multiple layers of identities were neither fully appropriating the new, caste-free 'Christian identity' nor willing to adhere to their ritual past. This tension enabled them to travel from a Christian consciousness to the Dalit consciousness, and even the other way. This was fuelled by the failure of both the church and the government in recognising and responding to the disadvantages faced by Dalit Christians.[9] Therefore, the multiple identities of Dalit Christians provided them space to express their resilience against the failure of both church and state in recognising the struggles of Dalit Christians. The multiple identities gave them space to celebrate their new identity, gave them a new affirmation of self, for they knew their faith in Christ had no compromise even though they were Hindu by law.

Multiple identities for Dalit Christians also offer a space for resilience against caste Christians and against Hindu Dalits. For Mary and her family, these multiple identities were an expression of resilience, for when the church had not recognised their struggles, their legal Hindu identity did not deter them from attending the church.

"The conversions of the lowest of the low were indeed a powerful and, at the same time, risky act of rebellion in the communally charged atmosphere of the late nineteenth and early twentieth centuries. It was not the material gains primarily which led the 'Chuharas' (in Punjab) to adopt Christianity, rather it was a transforming power of religious acceptance which impelled the lower caste people to shift to a religion looked at with suspicion by many in their own villages and cities. Christianity provided them with a new identity that made them change their names, eating habits and provided numerous other opportunities for self-betterment. The new religious identity in fact provided a cushion for the helpless Dalits in the highly oppressive caste structure of the village. In their struggle for survival, status and gain within the village the Dalits could now rely safely on the presence and influence of the Christian missionaries."[10] Therefore, for Dalit Christians, on the one hand, their multiple identities gave confidence in life in overcoming caste and its ramifications of oppression, and on the other, it helped them lead a life with hope of a better self and for the betterment of society.

Therefore, multiple identities for Dalit Christians gave them a new identity; it gave them an opportunity to express their resilience against all opposing forces in every quarter of life.

Conclusion

Layered multiple identities among Dalit Christians, while pushing them further into marginality, also provided a space to express their resilience against the insensitivity to their struggles towards liberation. For Dalit Christians, the Hindu identity is not their performed religious identity; and their experience as outcastes as a continuing identity is a challenge for the church and society to overcome their marginality and strengthen the resilience of Dalit Christians. These multiple identities of Dalit

Christians are a challenge for them, as they have to cope with the kinds of marginality they undergo. And in the backdrop of the church and the state being insensitive to the struggles of Dalit Christians, these multiple identities need to challenge the church and the Christian community in India to address and advocate for justice to Dalit Christians, to lobby for SC status for Christians of Dalit origin in order to establish justice and equality.

Dalit Christian struggle for justice is not just a Christian issue or just a Dalit issue, but a human rights issue and a constitutional issue in claiming their rights. These multiple identities of Dalit Christians also call on communities in India to affirm the right to choose a religion and profess a religion, for neither on the basis of caste nor on the basis of religion should discrimination stand. Dalit Christian identity is an identity to celebrate in the journey towards liberation. The marginality of Dalit Christians has pushed many Dalit Christians to martyrdom, for instance, in Kandhamal, Odisha; let me invoke strength from their faith and from their Dalit-ness.

Martyr O Dalit Christian martyr,
Your lives were made a satire,
By those with that saffron attire,
For some are killed by fire,
And some made as pyre,
On whom they had to play their lyre,
Of hatred, vengeance, death entire.

You stand as an inspiration,
your faith withstood the intimidation,
by forces of caste and condemnation.
may we carry your spirit of perspiration,
to keep up your aspiration.

Endnotes

[1] Ashok Kumar M. & Rowena Robinson, "Legally Hindu: Dalits Lutheran Christians of Coastal Andhra Pradesh," in Rowena Robinson & Joseph Marianus Kujur (eds), *Margins of Faith, Dalits & Tribal Christianity in India.* (New Delhi: Sage Publications, 2010),150 (Illustration modified).

[2] Chandra Mallampalli, *Christians and Public Life in Colonial South India.* (London: Routledge Curzon, 2006), 162-163.

[3] Ibid, 163-164.

[4] John C.B. Webster. *The Dalits Christians: A History.* (New Delhi: ISPCK, 1994), 128-129.

5 *In the Shadow of the Mahatma: Bishop V.S. Azariah and the Travails of Christianity in British India.* (Grand Rapids: Curzon Press, 2000), 252.

[6] Ashok Kumar M. & Rowena Robinson. "Legally Hindu: Dalits Lutheran Christians of Coastal Andhra Pradesh," in Rowena Robinson & Joseph Marianus Kujur (eds), *Margins of Faith, Dalits and Tribal Christianity in India.* (New Delhi: Sage Publications, 2010), 150.

[7] Khare, R.S. *The Untouchable as Himself: Ideology, Identity, and Pragmatism among the Lucknow Chamars.* (Cambridge: Cambridge University Press, 1984), 30.

[8] S.M. Michael, 2010. "Dalits Encounter with Christianity: Change & Continuity," in Rowena Robinson and Joseph Marianus Kujur (eds), *Margins of Faith, Dalits and Tribal Christianity in India.* (New Delhi: Sage Publications, 2010), 66.

[9] Chandra Mallampalli, *Christians and Public Life in Colonial South India.* (London: Routledge Curzon, 2006), 190.

[10] John Webster, "Who is a Dalits?" in S.M. Michael (ed.), *Dalits in Modern India: Vision and Values,* (New Delhi: Visthar, 1999), 103

Chapter 6

When my Grandma Annamma, Martin Luther & Pope Francis Meet:
A Conversational Reflection on Reformation

Narrator: *Read Acts 5:29 & Isaiah 7: 9b*

The global church celebrated 500 years of the Reformation in 2017, which served as an opportunity to rededicate and recommit our faith journey towards transforming our church and society. Here are three important people who have never met on earth, but in God's presence, where time and eternity meet, there is every possibility that these three people from three different historical and geographical backgrounds meet for a conversation. The three are Martin Luther, the sixteenth century reformer from Germany; Annamma, my grandmother and a first-generation Dalit Telugu Lutheran Christian from India, who lived in the twentieth century; Pope Francis, the current head of the Roman Catholic Church from Vatican in the twenty-first century.

Martin Luther (ML): Hi, grace and peace to you all; good to see you all here and wish I could have met you earlier in my days, but I know you lived well after my times. I understand both of you are very special, each in your own way, and it is the love of Christ that binds us together in unity, affirming our diversities. Praise be to God and God alone.

Pope Francis (PF): In the name of the Father, and of the Son and of the Holy Spirit. It is such a pleasure meeting you all here in the presence of God, where God is all and is present everywhere. Peace be with you Martin; peace be with you Annamma and peace be with you Narrator.

Annamma: *Namaskaram* (greetings) Luther, *Namaskaram* Pope Francis, and *Namaskaram* Narrator. I am thrilled to see you all here and it is such a joy for me to see you both here in this place of God. I heard of you, Luther, all my life from our missionaries and my dad, as a catechist, spoke about you so prominently, and heard of you Pope Francis from my grandchildren, and I am excited meeting you all.

PF: Father Martin, I still see you as our priest; I regret the decision to excommunicate you from our church then. But let me tell you that these 500 years of the Reformation and 50 years of Lutheran-Catholic dialogue has led us to move from conflict to communion, allowing God's Spirit to lead us thus far as co-members in the body of Christ.

When you nailed those 95 theses on the doors of Wittenberg Church on 31 October 1517, I have understood that my predecessors were terribly unhappy, and the mercury soared very high in their sphygmomanometer. Let me appreciate you for that courageous act, and as you know, it eventually turned out to be Reformation Day. What was it like?

ML: Should I call you His Grace or Fr. Francis, but I feel at home calling you Brother Francis. (The Pope nods his head with a smile.) Thank you for your appreciation, and wish you were the Pope then during my days, and I am glad good days have come for the church now. Allow me to reaffirm that the Reformation was an act of God, and I was only an instrument in the hands of the Holy Spirit. It was a sad state in the context of the church where gospel values were compromised and contaminated by power and authority; the Reformation of the church was a biblical necessity, a theological necessity and a contextual necessity of those times.

PF: I can understand that Martin, and glory be to God for your bravery and passion for the gospel. Now, let us invite our sister Annamma, whose name sounds like the name of St. Ann to me, to share what Reformation Day means to her.

Annamma: Thank you, Pope Francis. Martin Luther, though, is is miles away from our place in India and is distanced by about four centuries of time, his act of reformation is of great relevance to us. When the Lutheran missionaries brought us the gospel of Jesus Christ, they instilled in us a sense of self-dignity for we were considered 'untouchables' in our community for being born outside the caste system. Luther and his story were dear to us, for he spoke 'truth to the powers'; and Luther was identified as one among us, for he stood as an inspiration in overthrowing the corrupt powers of caste. We have owned Luther as our own. After becoming Christians, for us there were three important festivals. The first one was Christmas, the second was Reformation Day and the third was Easter. The Telugu translation of the word reformation is '*Mathodarana,*' which means 'restoration or upliftment of religion or religious system' or 're-establishment of religion.' Therefore, reformation was 'restoration' and 'upliftment,' which was our yearning for liberation from all oppressive religious practices—both within and outside of the church. We have grown enacting Luther's play from our childhood and aspired to make reformation a reality for our times, in our contexts. Faith alone, grace alone, Scripture alone are the foundations of our Christian living, and we believe that we are justified by faith in the love of Christ, and not by any religious rituals or works. We are liberated and saved by grace and not by any *karma* or acts.

ML: Very interesting to know about this, sister Annamma. I am glad you have taken the meaning of reformation to greater heights, broadening its scope, widening its horizon and deepening its meaning. As I said earlier, the Reformation is God's act, and God in God's grace activates and actualises reformation for God's people in varied and diverse contexts and stages of God's history. Praise be to God.

PF: Brilliant, sister Annamma, indeed praise be to God, for you have owned, reclaimed and re-enacted the story of Luther more profoundly than any others in the Global North. I now reckon that Luther and the Reformation has now become your story, your aspiration and your longing. Thank you, Annamma, for sharing this, and thank you, Martin, for initiating this. I now understand what it means to have 72 million Lutherans globally today in 2016 and why it is concentrated densely in the Global South. At this point, I should also say that we as Lutherans and Catholics have come closer on the 'doctrine of justification by faith,' for we acknowledge that this was part of the biblical theology of St. Paul, which precedes the early church father St. Augustine's teaching. I should also agree with the truth that 'salvation is not for sale.' We all collectively rejoice in God, for God has been gracious to us, for God's faithfulness endures from generation to generation.

Martin, let me now ask you, on 8 April 1521, when you were summoned to the Diet of Worms to reply to all the charges levelled against you, you were firm and stuck to what you had done and believed. What was that moment for you?

ML: Brother Francis, of all the things I did and of the things I wrote, how could you single out that moment at the Diet of Worms? I know you were trying to seek justification for my statement, "Here I stand." I was summoned to explain why I should not be excommunicated. I was asked not to rend the church, to retrieve my words and seek an apology. But my conviction in my Bible, the Word and the Spirit helped me stand by what I had believed, said and done. Therefore, let me repeat the same words I said then: "Since your majesty and your lordships desire a simple reply, I will answer without horns and teeth. Unless I am convicted by the Scripture and plain reason—I do not accept the authority of the Popes and the Councils for they had contradicted each other—my conscience is captive to the Word of God. I cannot and I will not recant anything, for to go against conscience is neither right nor safe. Here I stand, I cannot do otherwise, God help me. Amen."

Brother Francis, there I stand, and till eternity there I will stand.

PF: Thank you, Martin, we all knew that you were a tough guy and would not give up easily. Brilliant, you are an inspiring man, Martin. I knew your stand, but now let me ask sister Annamma, what is their Dalit Christian perspective on Luther's affirmation of 'Here I stand.'

Annamma: For Martin Luther, *Sola Fide* (faith alone) is a hermeneutic in unlocking 'justification,' for his context then was dominated by the rule of *Sola Roma* (Rome alone). Luther recited this verse "*If you do not stand firm in faith, you shall not stand at all*" from Isaiah 7: 9b, for he was always Scripture-centred and Word-focused. In this verse, there are three important facets of faith; first, the grounding of faith, which is in its 'standing'; second, the binding of faith, which is in its 'firmness'; and third, the longing of faith, which is 'fullness of life.' For it is our faith in a revolutionary Jesus Christ that inspires us to partake in the transformation of our society, for such a faith compels us to translate faith into praxis and roots us firmly in life—and life-giving mission.

In the context of caste oppression (*Sola Caste* or caste alone), we, Dalit Lutheran Christians, firmly believe that we do not accept the authority of caste, authority of powers, authority of oppressive texts, for we are liberated by the Word of God as revealed and personified in Jesus Christ. Here, we, as Dalit Christians, stand along with Luther, stand beside Luther and all people of God, in the faith of Jesus Christ, by the grace of God, with the Word of God; for nothing can separate and deter us from the reign of God that brings peace, justice and equality.

ML: Fantastic, sister Annamma, thank you for making me stand by my convictions in the Word, for making me stand along with you, for now I say, with people like you and your communities, I can stand and I will stand. Praise be to God.

PF: Thank you, sister Annamma for bringing in your powerful insights. I did hear about the plight of Dalit Christians and other such communities, for that was the reason time and again I stressed about 'Church of the poor' for I believed unless we are reincarnated as 'Church of the poor' we cannot bear witness to the values of the gospel. Moving 'From Conflict to Communion' for me is to ensure that liberation and justice becomes a reality for several people dying under the rubric of oppression. If as churches we can rise to that occasion, we can joyfully celebrate Reformation Day. We are called to reform our churches as 'Church of the poor' and I am sure Martin and all his people, be they Protestant or Evangelical or Charismatic, will join me in making this a reality, which is the need of the hour. Luther, you gave your message 500 years ago, and I have shared my own aspirations of the church; let us therefore ask sister Annamma to give us her reflection for this Reformation Day.

Annamma: Thank you, Pope Francis and Luther Sir, for being gracious in allowing me to speak on Reformation Day. Reformation for me, as I have said earlier, is 'hearing to speech' the often neglected, distorted, overlooked and even forgotten voices of the subalterns, the voices from the margins. Reformation for me is 'speaking truth to the powers for the cause of justice and peace. Reformation for me is a time of repentance for the callous attitudes of our churches and their leadership towards the needs of our people in the community; a time of repentance for those in power for we enjoy pomp and position at the expense of our vulnerable believers; a time of repentance for being silent about the unjust practices in our churches and for being insensitive to the exploitation of innocent people around us. Reformation for me is a time to give up my positions and privileges that I enjoy in the church, which is against the convictions of the gospel, and lead a life submitting ourselves at the feet of the cross in coherence with the crucified Christ.

The call of reformation today is to reject and defeat the authoritarian, ugly practice of caste and several other forms of it and pledge total obedience to our liberating God so that our public spaces of church, academy and society become zero-tolerant zones against discrimination. For Jesus, it was

'Roman Empire or Kingdom of God' and he chose the latter; for Luther, it was 'Rome or Christ' and he chose Christ over any other ecclesial authority; and today it is 'Caste or Christ,' and our ultimate choice is Christ over caste for it is now required in the reformation of our churches. 'Injustice done anywhere affects justice everywhere.'

Narrator: Thank you, sister Annamma, for your prophetic words, thank you brother Luther and thank you brother Francis for this interesting conversation. We submit to God and look to Him for His help so that our communities are transfigured, reformed and transformed.

Annamma: Should we not then close with one of Martin Luther's hymns that he had penned based on Psalm 46, for this song is our act of commitment and pledge. Let us all sing, "A Mighty Fortress is our God...."

Chapter 7

Dalits, Palestinians and Tribal Adivasis in their Quest for Common Struggle:
'We Look up to the hills, from where will our help come?'

Introduction

James Cameron's blockbuster movie *Avatar* transports viewers to the hanging mountains and dreamscape of planet Pandora. Famous theologian Kwok Pui-lan, in her review of the film titled "*Avatar*: A Subversive Reading of the Bible?," writes: "In *Avatar*, planet Pandora is not only a land of milk and honey, but also has a large reserve of a precious metal unobtanium. The avatar of Jake is sent as a messenger to ask the natives to relocate so that the humans can mine the unobtanium. Jake learns the native ways, falls in love with one of them, and becomes so identified with the natives such that he helps them to fight against the colonizers."[1] The movie invites us to look at the world from the point of the indigenous people, the Adivasis, the Tribals, and the Dalits—to see the beauty of our interconnected way of life and learn about our culture.

When contextual articulations of faith narratives are at a crossroads, when experiences of 'walk the talk' among God-human-talk are perceived as competitors rather than collaborators, when such expressive talks fail to make their relevance felt, an attempt to bring together local critical faith articulations for a walk becomes immanent. Such an attempt's motive is to build bonds of solidarity for dialogue and mutual understanding. In response to a recent invitation of 'Come and See,' my journey to Palestine made me realise that I am on an Emmaus journey, as a co-pilgrim in the journey towards justice. As co-pilgrims, we have a common destiny; as co-pilgrims we share our struggles by listening and sharing; as co-pilgrims we have embarked on a journey of hope, for we affirm in a God of hope who is willing to journey along with us; and as co-pilgrims we strengthen our commitment and resolve when hope seems blurred. Building friendships of solidarity is a step forward in realising our dream of liberation and justice. Here I have attempted to highlight contextual realities, bring out the resonances from our Dalit/Adivasi ground zero and that of the Palestinian indigenous issues, and thereby have attempted to work out a theological response from a young Indian Dalit ecumenical learner.

Our Common Milieu: Resonances from Ground Zero

Israel happens to be the cradle of three major world religions—Judaism, Christianity and Islam, and thereby receives the attribute 'holy' land. India, like Israel, also happens to be the cradle of four other major religions—Hinduism, Buddhism, Jainism and Sikhism, besides being the birthplace of many ancient indigenous religions and spiritualities, and thereby brings holiness to her land. In both these holy sites, unholy acts have been practised and perpetuated; in one land, indigenous Palestinians have become victims, and in the other, Dalits and Adivasis have been the worst victims of discrimination. In this pursuit, allow me to bring to light three issues for our discussion here.

The unholy sights in these holy sites: Walls and Gates

Journeying through the streets of Palestine led me to anger, distress, disappointment and frustration. The perpetuation of segregation and separation by Israel through their cruel occupation and the confiscation of Palestine lands by building walls, fences and gates to divide and disperse their towns and villages are beyond imagination in this so-called 'holy land.' We have foreign 'settlers' on mountain tops guarded by security forces and native inhabitants of the land of Palestine in gated communities. The humiliation of Palestinians and the discrimination and human right violations against them know no bounds.

These sights are not new for a country like India. Indian societies have been divided in the name of caste for ages; we have dominant caste groups living around the temple, inside the village, whereas those who are born outside the caste, the Dalits, living segregated outside the villages as communities. We have invisible gates around these Dalit communities, which are very strong and deep, for they are built on the grounds of purity and pollution. There are several examples to illustrate how Dalits have been denied entry to dominant caste localities and how they are humiliated and ostracised when they have attempted to walk through their paths. Oppression of Dalits have become subtle and aggressive these days, for there has been an increasing violence against Dalits with several killings, rapes and arrests; many go unreported, while others go unattended.

Dalits are forced to work as manual scavengers to clean human excreta with their bare hands, which again is an occupation based on caste discrimination. The cries of Dalit women are beyond description, for they have been oppressed in the name of gender, class and caste. Walls of division in cemeteries, walls in churches, walls among different communities are all a reality today in the name of caste.

The Hydra of Zionism and Hindutva: Hatred and Violence

Like Zionism in Israel, which calls for one nation and one religion, a Hindu cultural fundamental group in India which subscribes to the ideology of Hindutva calls for India to be one Hindu *rashtra* (state) with one Hindu religion. Both these trends are dangerous and venomous, for they have been attacking and persecuting religious minorities in both our countries, particularly Muslims and Christians. Globalisation is hand in glove with these ideologies, for it promotes homogenisation and counters all forms of diversities. It tries to bring uniformity and not unity. These ideologies promulgate violence, for they want to achieve their goal of 'one-ness' by any means, breeding exclusivism and absolutism. Once again, it is Palestinians and Dalits who have been the worst victims of these ideologies. Their ideologues perpetuate violence, encourage hatred and make inflammatory speeches and hate campaigns against the minorities. The state governments are soft towards them.

Saffronisation of education, extrajudicial killings, state-sponsored violence, unjust trials in courts of law, extraconstitutional authorities to rabbis and *swamiji*s are all part of the package of these ideologies. Demolitions of places of worship (on 6 December 1992, Babri Masjid, was demolished in Ayodhya by these forces), destruction of sites of spiritual importance, attacks on properties and places of minorities are the outcome of all these. The Kandhamal episode in Odisha explains vividly the cruel face of Hindutva on Dalits and Tribals. Both these ideologies are like *Hydra*, a snake from Greek mythology, which has several faces and they crop up according to the need of the uncertainty that exists.

Plundering of lands & natural resources: Groaning and Pain

The Israeli settlers and the dominant caste/class groups in India plunder the lands of Palestinians and that of Dalits and Adivasis, respectively. In Israel, in the name of God, in the name of force and for the cause of security, they plunder the land. In India, in the name of development, in the name of bonded labour and for the cause of prosperity, they plunder the land. Such plunder makes communities landless and powerless, for their spiritualities and their sentiments are intertwined with their land. The outsiders take away the lands and control the resources of the original inhabitants. This has displaced these communities, and turn them into refugees and strangers in their own land. Not only are these communities affected by the plundering, but mother earth groans in pain and suffering due to the insensitivity of those in power towards her. The rich green lands are turned into deserts and thereby create ecological imbalances.

The unholy alliances of patriarchy, capitalism, casteism, etc., make for a vicious circle of oppression. Among various vertices of injustices around us, injustices done to mother earth and injustices done to those living in the margins of the society—Palestinians, Dalits, Tribals, women, migrants—particularly call our attention as those interested in peace and justice issues. Both creation and the people in the margins mutually share their pain and have been yearning for justice and peace, here and right now!

A case at hand that shows our predicament is Britain's Vedanta Resources, the multinational bauxite mining company, which has pitched its tent in Odisha, one of the eastern states of India. In August 2010, the Supreme Court of India allowed Vedanta Resources to mine bauxite in the Niyamgiri Hills of Odisha. The mined bauxite would feed the company's proposed $800-million alumina refinery in Kalahandi district and an aluminium smelter project, costing Rs. 70 billion, in Jharsuguda district of Odisha. This project is going to damage the livelihood and the environment of more than 8,000 Dongria Khond Adivasi people. Thanks to the persistent resistance by people's movements to this project, this multinational company was sent out of these hills in Niyamgiri. The Na'vi in the film *Avatar,* the Dalits of Chengara in Kerala, the Palestinians and the Dongria Khond Adivasis in India share several common issues of justice and peace.

From the above contextual realities, deciphering the signs of our times, one can draw parallels between Palestinian and Dalit and Adivasi struggles and observe several commonalities among the struggles. Here are a few of them:

a. They happen to be the indigenous, local inhabitants of their own lands, yet they do not have their lands with them. In both cases, land and natural resources are owned and controlled by those in power.

b. They have been segregated and are oppressed either in the name of nationality and religious identity or in the name of caste and ethnicity.

c. Their oppression has religious sanction and religious scriptures have been used in justifying the oppression.

d. These communities do not enjoy religious liberty, for they are denied access to the holy places; Palestinians on the pretext of security, and Dalits on the pretext of pollution. (In most Hindu temples, at the holy of holies, a signboard reads "Non-Hindus are not allowed into this holy place.")

e. These communities are humiliated and subjected to various kinds of torture, creating a fear psychosis among them.

f. These communities have been refugees in several quarters, for emigration and migration among these people have been on the rise.

g. These communities have been the victims of unjust laws and policies, for international human rights laws are not applied and implemented by their respective governments.

h. These communities have been victims of historical injustices, victims of ongoing violence and human rights violations.

i. These communities have been viewed by international communities as a matter of humanitarian aid or objects of charity and have never been analysed as subjects of justice and peace.

j. Palestinian Christians and Dalit Christians have been denied their constitutional rights. In the case of Palestinian Christians in Jerusalem, their right to living is slowly being denied, and Dalit Christians are denied affirmative actions like the Scheduled Caste status from the government on becoming Christians. Many schemes and policies for Dalit empowerment are not being channelised and utilised.

In search of our Common Ideology: "We look up to the hills, from where will our help come?"

The above situations set our chosen text Psalm 121:1 in context to ponder and delve upon. Psalms 120-134, popularly called 'songs of ascent,' were used as hymns that were sung by pilgrims as they gathered at Jerusalem during the appointed feasts for the whole nation. As the pilgrims journeyed to Jerusalem, which stands at an elevation, their eyes were continuously upon the hills, for the hills were their solace and destiny to which they were journeying. The pilgrims anticipated help, calling on the accompaniment of the divine, which the psalmist records in the first verse of the Psalm. The assurance from the divine is recorded in the succeeding verses.

Taking cognisance of the realities of the Adivasi people, our indigenous brothers and sisters and their struggles, their ongoing campaigns to affirm self-dignity and their fight for justice, allow me to reflect upon the given verse from the perspective of marginalised communities. Our people's daily prayer is, 'We look up to the hills, from where will our help come?' In a context where hills are broken down for profit, and where forests are cut down for selfishness and greed, particularly in Palestine where lands are occupied and when the indigenous people are made aliens and foreigners, where will our help come from?

Hills represent strength

For the indigenous people in Niyamgiri, Odisha, and for several others like them elsewhere in the world, hills are symbolic representations of their life systems. For generations they have lived on the hills, and their livelihood, their sentiments, their religion, their culture, their beliefs, their civilisation and their value systems all are interwoven with the hills. Their strength is their relationship with the hills; their stronghold is in their association with the hills, the fauna and the flora there. Life for the Dongria Khond people is their hills in Niyamgiri, and they cannot accept life without their hills.

'We look up to the hills, from where will our help come?' continues to be the echo that is heard from that hill, and help shall certainly come from the God of the hills. 'A mighty fortress is our God...' is the hope against hope with which our people live, and the God of justice who cares for the displaced and the indigenous people shall come in rescue of them. Hills do not represent power, rather they are part of God's creation and their strength lies in being a help to others, be it in causing rain, be it in protecting the forests or be it in giving a livelihood to people.

Hills provide succour

People who are forced to leave and are displaced from their original inhabitations continuously look towards the hills for they know out of the hills will come sunshine and out of the hills their help will come. Modern technology may blast the hill into pieces to dig out the ore, but the will of those on that hill is so strong that no force on earth can disunite or shatter them, for they affirm that their hills are their strength. Hills serve as healers for these, our people; they give succour and comfort to the wounded and tired. The natural ecosystems give them fresh air of healing, for there is interdependence of humans and creation in its perfect balance.

The LXX (Septuagint, the Greek translation of the Old Testament) has the Greek work *boetheia* for 'help' in Psalm 121:1 and it is used in Acts 27:17 to mean 'supporting cables';

therefore the support to hold together in all harmony comes from the hills, which is the belief and comfort of the people there. God of comfort, who succours God's people through the presence of the Holy Spirit, is the driving force for the people who are fighting against the mining industry.

Hills reassure solidarity

When the rights of the indigenous people are violated, and violence against them is rampant, the hills unite people to stand for justice at any cost. The indigenous peoples' lives are at risk, and they are in need of support and voice from across the world for justice. Hills, which see that nature is in solidarity with the people there and that the people are in solidarity with nature, establish a strong bond of kinship among them. Therefore, when one is in trouble, the other comes in solidarity with the other. Thanks to all the social activists fighting for justice and the Church of England, which has withdrawn its investment support in this particular firm for violating the human rights of the indigenous people in Odisha. God of justice, who has created the heavens and the earth, builds communities of peace and solidarity for the good of creation. God holds together all creation and humans, who work hand in hand. Solidarity comes from God, for God is the local inhabitant with the people on the hills, and we need to accompany the victims of injustice towards liberation and justice.

Signposts for Moving Forward

- Time has come to recover the Bible. A joint Dalit-Adivasi-Palestinian reading of the Bible needs to be worked out and projected in order to provide a perspective to our struggles. For instance, books like Nehemiah needs to be reread, for most times we read it as 'come let's build the walls' not knowing the adverse impact it has for Palestinians. We need to deconstruct such readings and add new meanings like building bridges among people today.

- Situate and locate our struggles in the Asian setting, for our struggles are Asian struggles striving for Asian solutions and therefore we need to expand our networks among Asian countries for a profound solidarity for our struggles.

- Inculcate 'earth-centred spiritualities.' Let issues of land be the common denominator for our struggles, for an interfacing of Dalit liberation theology, Adivasi theology and Palestine liberation theology is the need of the day to work out common strategies and methodologies for liberation. Encourage Dalit-Tribal-Palestine theological dialogue. For example, the Chengara land struggle in Kerala and how 5,000 Dalits have taken over land by pitching tents there.

- Develop exchanges between communities. Student social forums should invite Palestine youth to speak and to learn from our contexts.

- Expose our local tour operators offering pilgrimage to Palestine to the realities of the land and encourage alternative tourism.

- May the International Day in Solidarity with Palestine on November 29 be popularised, calling the attention of local congregations to the Palestinian problem with necessary homilies and liturgies. Assigning one Sunday as *kairos* Palestine Sunday and calling on all to observe it globally shall strengthen our resolve.

- Let the Dalit, Adivasi and Palestine issues be projected as justice issues, faith issues and not as mere diakonial issues.

Conclusion

At a time when huge structures of churches are being built across the country, at a time when the orthodoxy of the churches limits us from performing certain rituals within the four walls of the so-called sanctuaries, at a time when churches criticise each other on the basis of doctrines and dogmas, at a time when we as churches are stuck with our orthodoxy, it is certainly a challenge to turn towards an orthopraxial understanding of the church. How practical are we as churches? Does our existence as churches have any meaning and relevance to the society in which we live?

Churches today need to be like the hills, where human beings, the flora and fauna and the entire creation live in mutual harmony with each other (not like a pinnacle of power and prestige). The church needs to give strength to those indigenous people, for they look up to the hills of churches, which objectively need to be homes of justice. The church is the place where succour and comfort is granted to those victims of human rights violations, and it is time that we as church rose up to the occasion of giving succour and tranquillity to communities around. When people look up to the hills of churches, are we able to come in aid of them? The church is a place that reassures solidarity, for we need to journey with the marginalised and the oppressed towards their destined liberation. No matter what the identity of the people is and no matter what religious affirmations people practice, if the struggle is for justice, the church needs to be in solidarity with them even at the expense of their lives. People look up to the hills of churches for solidarity, where will the help come from.

The Lutheran World Federation in its General Assembly in July 2010 discussed the theme 'Give us today our daily bread.' If our churches can be Bethlehem, the house of bread, we can make our churches more relevant for our times. As we join in the breaking of the bread, let us forget our orthodox church traditions and affirmations and cling to orthopraxis, where we would be willing to be broken for the cause of our communities; for only by being broken can we satiate the hunger of many around. It is not hilltop churches that we are in need of, but churches that serve as hills of strength, succour and solidarity. The will of the churches should be to be hills of help. Let us as a church wake up to see the grim realities around and let us commit ourselves to be in solidarity with the people of Dongria Khond in saving the hills of Niyamgiri in Odisha and be a channel of liberation and justice. We may be distanced by space and time from Niyamgiri, from Palestine, but our sensitivity towards the indigenous people and their struggles needs to be taken into the cognisance of our church lives, for we need to garner support in favour of the people by expressing our total support to this cause of life and justice.

Let me conclude by echoing the clarion call that was made by the National Council of Churches in India as an attempt in articulating *Kairos*-India at its National Ecumenical Conference on Justice for Dalits in October 2010:

> As Christians we claim to reflect the mind of Christ but we are vested in the logic of caste. Jesus says *'no one can serve two masters, for a slave will either love the one and hate the other, or be devoted to one and despise the other'* (Matthew 6: 24). In a context of caste division, caste discrimination and caste violence we announce from the rooftop: 'No one can serve Christ and

caste!' We also confess that in our caste-infested world 'we have decided to follow Christ.' Empowered by a deep faith in God, who binds us into communion, who frees us for justice and who heals us towards wholeness, we join together to live faithfully as disciples of Christ in India today. This involves public confession of our complicity in the sin of casteism, reaffirmation of our faith in a God of justice and a radical commitment to solidarity with those crushed under the weight of the caste system.

In line with that tone, if caste is pronounced as sin, occupation in the Palestinian and Adivasi contexts needs to be pronounced boldly as sin; for we are all called like prophet Jeremiah, "See, today I appoint you over nations and kingdoms to uproot and tear down, to destroy and overthrow, to build and to plant" (Jer 1:10). May the walls of division in this land be torn down and destroyed so that peace and justice shall flow like ever-flowing streams. Today we need prophets like Jonah, who after his experience in the belly of a fish, proclaimed a fast that challenges the polis of his day, the polity of his day and the prophecy of his day, thereby saving the territory and city of Nineveh. Jonah truly is the first prophet of his kind who had a blend of the Dalit-Palestine ethos in achieving justice. The Student Christian Movement of India pledged its support to the Palestinian struggles for justice; when its General Committee met recently, we wrestled on the theme "Blessed are those in the margins, for they shall inherit the land," drawing parallels from our Dalit/Adivasi experiences.

I thought young Joseph would be there welcoming
but it was young men with guns at checkpoints incoming
I thought young Mary would be there welcoming
But it was young women with guns at checkpoints incoming
I thought then it would be the manger that's welcoming
but shockingly, it was the huge concrete wall of separation.

a wall of division
a wall of segregation
a wall of occupation
a wall of humiliation
a wall of discrimination
Making the birth of Jesus' place invisible.

O Jesus, come now to be born again here
to break these walls of domination
to tear down these walls of demonisation
to break open the cruel hearts of oppressions
to restore liberation and peace on this earth
and to bring glad tidings of joy to all these people
Come Jesus, and come now!

In hope I leave, only to return to see Joseph, Mary and
baby Jesus—in all freedom—in this land.

Endnote

[1] https://religiondispatches.org/iavatari-a-subversive-reading-of-the-bible/

PART III

The Location of *Dalitekklesia:*
Public Witness

This part of the discussions is about public witness which
helps in our reimagining of a church from below

Chapter 8

Remembering Ilavarasan, Interrogating Casteism:
Reimagining Christian Public Witness in India

The fourth of July 2013 was a day stained with blood from the brutal murder of a young Ilavarasan by the unholy alliance of caste and politics; it was a day when Ilavarasan and his love were defeated by the cruel forces of caste and patriarchy and it was a day when caste and power held its head high by murdering Ilavarasan. Ilavarasan, a young icon for love and liberation, is no more alive, but his life, death and memory continue to challenge each of us to oust and drive away caste from our vicinities, for caste and its tentacles are deadly and disastrous. Remembering Ilavarasan is a contextual, sociological and theological necessity, for his death happens at a time when each of us are complacent in our journey of faith; and his life and death is a wake-up call to the community at large to interrogate the evil called casteism and to explore whether our faith has any relevance and implication in our Christian public witness. Here is an attempt to analyse the given situation from a young, Dalit, pastoral and ecumenical perspective, thereby proposing certain directives in our pilgrimage of faith. This is not an extensive and an exhaustive analysis but an attempt in searching for meaning to life, justice and peace.

Contextual Analysis

Here is the report of the incident taken from *kafila.com*, for there have been several reports done by various journalists on the whole episode of Ilavarasan and each carried its own shade and perspective. This reporting, which I found to be objective, is brought forth for our analysis.

> *It was a few weeks after his marriage with Divya, a girl belonging to the caste of Vanniars, a Most Backward Caste in the official description of Tamil Nadu Government, in October 2012, [that] Divya's father was found dead allegedly having committed suicide due to the "dishonour" caused by his daughter's marriage. Making the suicide an excuse, the Vanniyars organized riots in which three Dalit hamlets, about 250 houses, were destroyed. The scale of violent destruction caught the national attention and so did the love story behind the riots. The young couple earned a media profile while trying to live in peace beyond the reach of the raging Vanniyar caste men. It was fated that was not to be. The Vanniar caste leaders used Divya's mother to temporarily separate Divya from Ilavarasan by using the well-known tactics of emotional blackmail. They then broke the communication link between Ilavarasan and Divya. When Ilavarasan saw Divya in the court on the first of July, Divya told the court that she would live with Ilavarasan after convincing her mother. Divya's lawyer, however, managed to make her tell the press that she is separated from Ilavarasan forever. Ilavarasan, on the other hand, told India Today, that he was highly hopeful of reuniting with Divya. After two days, he was found dead near a railway track in broad daylight. Given this history, the news had some potential to shock people.*
>
> *The police said it was a case of suicide by throwing oneself in front of a running train since the body with a split head was found near the track. Very soon it was contested by everyone that it*

was impossible for the body to remain intact except for the split head if it was run over by a train. Nor is it imaginable that a body would only be thrown a few feet off by a speeding train if it had hit the train; it was found just within three feet from the track. Amidst gathering protests in Dharmapuri and elsewhere, the government typically tried to re-iterate the suicide theory fearing a large-scale caste conflict. The clumsy attempts by the police and administration have only incited more passion and the cry for justice is widespread now. The court has ordered a second post-mortem by the medical professionals from the AIIMS, Delhi.[1]

And they confirmed that it was a death caused by being hit by a running train, whereas the Railways made an internal inquiry and found that no one had died on 4 July in an accident.

Ilavarasan's death on a railway track will remind of the suspicious death of 30-year-old Rizwanur Rahman in Kolkata in 2007, under similar circumstances, after he married industrialist Ashok Todi's daughter. What is it then that connects Haryana to Kolkata and Tamil Nadu? Besides the obvious Indian connection, there is the immense social, political and economic pressure brought to bear on young adults in love. For Dalits, the stifling endogamy of the caste system is just one marker of discrimination and oppression.[2]

Ilavarasan is not alive today to share his story of discrimination and pressure he and his entire village had to endure for falling in love with a dominant caste girl and then marrying her. The incidents that followed his inter-caste marriage are gruesome and horrendous. Herewith is a brief analysis of the whole Ilavarasan incident; all these themes are interwoven and it would be difficult to take each one in isolation for the trajectories run across themes.

- **Violence against Dalit communities** erupted as an immediate follow-up of an inter-caste marriage; nearly 250 houses were burnt by dominant caste communities, ransacking whole lives of Dalit communities.

- There has been an **anti-Dalit hate campaign** in the aftermath of the inter-caste marriage. The dominant caste groups started to speak against inter-caste marriages, trying to say that Dalit boys were wooing caste girls for their wealth; a Pattali Makkal Katchi (PMK) leader was even quoted as saying, "Dalit boys now wear jeans and goggles, T-shirts and [brandish] cellphones." Educated Hindu caste boys distributing pamphlets propagating against inter-caste marriages is a follow-up of Ilavarasan's death in Tamil Nadu today.

- There is a political conspiracy in the whole episode; appeasing a majority community by spitting venom against Dalit communities, all for the sake of electoral politics and **constructing an electoral constituency in the name of a dominant caste.**

- **The social mobility of Dalits in the economic sphere** has become a sore point for dominant caste groups. It was also opined that, "The recent rise in the socio-economic condition of Dalits, sections of whom are moving from farm labour into various forms of urban or migrant work, has created a situation of conflict with the landowning backward classes. This has occasionally resulted in aggressive violence against Dalits in several parts of Tamil Nadu in the past decade, with the Dalits facing attacks largely from the landed backward classes—Vanniyars in the north, Kallars in the south."[3]

- There is **an increase in the number of suicides of Dalit youth**; be it due to discrimination in educational institutions, be it due to honour killings, be it because of the corporate competitive empire, the saga continues.

- The **nexus between caste and politics, caste and patriarchy, and caste and power** is what is visualised as the common denominator in this whole incident.

These themes bring us to some unanswered questions with which we have to struggle and grapple with in our context today.

a. How do we understand the Dalit politics of 'love'? Does not a Dalit youth have freedom of choice to love a person; why are they discriminated, ostracised, beaten and even killed (some are even falsely reported as suicides) when they fall in love with people from other communities?

b. Can we attempt a sociological and a theological audit on the given incident and look for avenues in revisiting the whole enterprise of inter-caste marriages for what they offer in overcoming the casteist mindsets in our country?

c. Why have we as a community of faith been silent and absent when incidences of injustice prevail right in our own localities? Does not our faith challenge us to address issues of caste and other similar unjust practices prevalent in our communities?

These are some unending questions that came to light when Ilavarasan's murder took place.

Remembering Ilavarasan

Memories of Ilavarasan have started to fade from the minds of people, of his death and his struggle to overcome castesist forces. With lots of other news making headlines, not much is reported about his death, the post-mortem, what happened to Divya and how she is coping with the reality of her husband being not alive, how is the whole Dalit community in Natham in Tamil Nadu coping with this reality? There has been an attempt by the dominant communities to wipe away the memory of Ilavarasan from the minds and consciousness of all.

Remembering Ilavarasan for the sake of a memorial service is not the intention, neither is it to read a good tribute or his obituary; rather, it is to awaken us from our slumber of insensitivity towards the practices of caste, which are subtle but cruel these days. Ilavarasan's life, love, struggle for justice and death calls for a *kairos* moment in our lives to stand up for the cause of justice in the context of the venomous caste system.

a. **Ilavarasan is remembered as a Rosa Parks of our times:** Most of us would have read of the act of Rosa Parks, the African-American civil rights activist, on 1 December 1955, when by her act of not giving up her seat to white passengers on a bus in Alabama, she turned the attention of the world towards the plights of the Black Americans. Park's acts of defiance and the Montgomery Bus Boycott became important symbols of the modern civil rights movement.

   Likewise is Ilavarasan's act of enduring the domination of casteist forces, his courage to propagate to the world that love transcends all barriers, including caste, and that moment in which he would not succumb to the pressures of denial and discrimination. Ilavarasan's life calls for responsible citizenry to wake up and contest the demon of our times, casteism. His life is a testimony of courage, his love is a symbol of resilience and resistance against caste forces, and his death is a call to action by all those silent and insensitive people to overcome the evil of caste. Lest many more Ilavarasan's are murdered, let us wake up to prevent it by resisting the forces of caste.

b. **Ilavarasan is remembered as a Nelson Mandela of our contexts:** Recently we celebrated Nelson Day, on the 18 July, which is a day to promote a culture of peace among people on his birthday. Mandela's resolve to end apartheid, his commitment to his own community and his courage in fighting the racist regime and racist attitudes paved the way for an awakening among world communities and thereby paved the way for an anti-racist, anti-apartheid community with equality and justice.

Likewise, Ilavarasan's resolve to overcome casteist forces was witnessed by his courage of marrying a dominant caste girl, knowing the consequences of such a marriage. He was bold to live for his love, bold to live for his commitment, bold in living for his values, and has now inspired several young people to be bold in their own belief systems. His life is an example of the commitment to love; not worrying about his own life, he wanted to remain a true lover, and he did remain a true lover till his last breath. Ilavarasan's life is a witness to the commitment of love and a wake-up call to several of us to be committed in our values for liberation, which is to be attained by love. Lest many more Ilavarasans are murdered, let us wake up to prevent such murders by affirming love in life, which is beyond the boundaries of caste.

c. **Ilavarasan is remembered as Archbishop Oscar Romero in our belief systems:** Archbishop Oscar Romero was assassinated on 24 March 1980 while celebrating a mass in El Salvador, for his vociferous stand against the unjust class system, for his commitment to the cause of human rights, for his gospel to the poor. He is remembered for his outright attacks on the unjust empire and its regime and was bold in applying faith to the given context.

Likewise, Ilavarasan is remembered as the Archbishop Oscar Romero of our belief systems, who became a martyr for the cause of justice. Ilavarasan's life speaks for his vociferous stand against caste, for he too became a martyr for the cause of love and liberation. Imagine the kind of stress and trauma he had to undergo when his villages were attacked and houses burnt, just for standing committed in life and love. Imagine the kind of pressure he would have had when the strong political class and caste took up his issue in order to denounce inter-caste marriages. It would have been beyond bounds of tolerance to express the kind of suffering and oppression he had to face. Since he withstood all the unjust pains for the cause of life and love, he was murdered, and he became a martyr for the cause of love, for the cause of the anti-caste liberation movement.

I know it is hard to draw comparisons with other personalities, for that would undervalue the potential and the commitment of Ilavarasan. However, my point in remembering him is that he was murdered and he draws the attention of the world community to wake up to fight against caste in all forms and practices like other champions of justice did.

Interrogating Casteism

In the given context of the brutal murder of Ilavarasan as a victim of caste politics and caste power, it is high time we interrogated and analysed the caste intricacies that exist in our society today. Unless we are bold in naming the demon, it would be difficult to become agents casting away the demon of caste today.

Felix Wilfred, in one his essays 'Subalterns and Ethical Auditing,' explains the "hypocritical silence on caste." He says that caste is observed scrupulously by the elite upper class and caste groups; they still do not want to speak about or want to be seen talking about caste. He goes on to explain that "like the proverbial cat that has nine lives, caste takes on ever new avatars which makes it difficult to censure and bring under ethical auditing." He further goes to say, "The Dalits speak about caste without inhibition, because they want to exorcize this demon. On the other hand, upper castes want to be silent on caste in public and derive all the benefits and power through it."[4] Therefore the dominant castes only enjoy the benefits of and from the caste system and remain silent even in times of violence such as the killing of Ilavarasan and the ransacking of 250 Dalit houses. It is a convenient choice by all people to remain silent and thereby see that caste and its ramifications are alive, inviting violence and oppression of on Dalits.

Though there are varied hydra forms of caste in the twenty-first century, given the limitation of space and time, allow me to discuss briefly the dynamics in inter-caste marriages. Why has there been a lot of opposition to inter-caste marriages? In a pluralistic society like India, it would be inevitable to witness inter-caste, inter-religious, inter-regional marriages, for we live in a country of pluralities.

Exposing the Perils of Endogamy

The news after Ilavarasan's murder is that educated caste Hindu youth campaigned against inter-caste marriages. "I have known girls (friends and relatives) of our community fall in love with boys from other communities and marry them. It not only affected them but also their families that were pushed to shame from which they were unable to recover even many years after the marriage," says P. Karthik (22), an engineering professional, in a report in *The Hindu*.[5] The report further quotes him as saying, "India is known for its rich tradition that is preserved by communities in the country over the years. Inter-caste marriages will put an end to this tradition." How can these educated young people of India today affirm endogamy by saying it preserves a rich tradition and that they fear inter-caste marriages would break the exclusive oppressive traditions? It was further opined: "Inter-caste marriages have always been resented by casteists all over India—parents, caste bodies and political parties. The recent death of Ilavarasan, a young Dalit man in Tamil Nadu's Dharmapuri district, highlights once again the vice-like grip of caste prejudice."[6]

One can notice the expressions of power in preserving endogamy. Caste groups try to remain unaffected and unpolluted by lower castes coming into their families and therefore impose several restrictions, upon their women particularly and oppose inter-caste marriages.

Inter-caste Marriages as Spaces for Anti-caste Practices

Inter-caste marriages have been a practice for more than a century in India, and several social reformers have advocated the cause of such marriages. These kinds of marriages have become expressions and spaces for anti-caste practices, and have always been a step in overcoming vicious caste practices. It is worth noting that the first inter-caste marriage was proposed and done by Jotirao Phule and Savitribai Phule, who championed the cause of Dalit liberation and women's empowerment.

> *The first inter-caste marriage in modern India took place on 4 February 1889. On this date, Yashwant and Radha (alias Laxmi) got married. Yaswant was the adopted son of Jotirao and Savitribai Phule. Radha was daughter of Gyanoba Krishnaji Sasane. This marriage was the first 'Satyashodhaki' (truth seeker society) marriage. Savitribai herself bore all the expenses on this historic occasion. This method of marriage, similar to a registered marriage, is still prevalent in many parts of India. These marriages were opposed by priests and 'bhatjis' (Brahmans) all over the country and they also went to court on this matter. Savitribai and Jotirao had to face severe difficulties but that did not deter them from their path. The Satyashodhak marriage required the bridegroom to take an oath of giving education and equal rights to women. The 'mangalashtake' (the Mantras chanted at the time of the wedding) were to be sung by the bride and the bridegroom themselves, and these were in the form of pledges made by the bride and the groom to each other. To ensure that they got better acquainted with each other and with each other's likes and dislikes, Savitribai had made Radha stay in the Phule household even before the marriage took place. She also made provisions for Radha's education.*
>
> *In India, inter caste marriages were publicly encouraged and supported by politicians such as C. N. Annadurai, the first Chief Minister of Tamil Nadu, and social activists such as Periyar E. V. Ramasamy, Raghupathi Venkataratnam Naidu and Manthena Venkata Raju.*[7]

Jotirao Phule and Savitribai Phule chose inter-caste marriages as an expression to create spaces for anti-caste practices, and these inter-caste marriages, they believed, are the steps forward to champion Dalit liberation.

Ambedkar on Inter-caste Marriages

As a social political reformer, Dr. Babasaheb Ambedkar ushered in a new era in India's sociopolitical history. On the front page of his book *What Congress and Gandhi have done to the Untouchables*, Ambedkar quoted the Greek philosopher Thucydides who said, "It may be your interest to be our master, but how can it be ours to be your slaves?"[8] Ambedkar was bold in questioning the validity of the caste system and made Dalits to affirm their rights in their struggle for equality. Ambedkar always said that inter-dining and inter-caste marriages were ways to eradicate and annihilate caste from our societies.

In his classic "Annihilation of Caste," Ambedkar explains:

The real remedy for breaking Caste is inter-marriage. Nothing else will serve as the solvent of Caste.... You are right in holding that Caste will cease to be an operative farce only when inter-dining and inter-marriage have become matters of common course. You have located the source of the disease. But is your prescription the right prescription for the disease? Ask yourselves this question; Why is it that a large majority of Hindus do not inter-dine and do not inter-marry? Why is it that your cause is not popular? There can be only one answer to this question and it is that inter-dining and inter-marriage are repugnant to the beliefs and dogmas which the Hindus regard as sacred. Caste is not a physical object like a wall of bricks or a line of barbed wire which prevents the Hindus from co-mingling and which has, therefore, to be pulled down.

Caste is a notion; it is a state of the mind. The destruction of Caste does not therefore mean the destruction of a physical barrier. It means a notional change. Caste may be bad. Caste may lead to conduct so gross as to be called man's inhumanity to man. All the same, it must be recognized that the Hindus observe Caste not because they are inhuman or wrongheaded. They observe Caste because they are deeply religious. People are not wrong in observing Caste. In my view, what is wrong is their religion, which has inculcated this notion of Caste. If this is correct, then obviously the enemy, you must grapple with, is not the people who observe Caste, but the Shastras which teach them this religion of Caste. Criticizing and ridiculing people for not inter-dining or inter-marrying or occasionally holding inter-caste dinners and celebrating inter-caste marriages, is a futile method of achieving the desired end. The real remedy is to destroy the belief in the sanctity of the Shastras. How do you expect to succeed, if you allow the Shastras to continue to mold the beliefs and opinions of the people? Not to question the authority of the Shastras, to permit the people to believe in their sanctity and their sanctions and to blame them and to criticize them for their acts as being irrational and inhuman is a incongruous way of carrying on social reform. Reformers working for the removal of untouchability including Mahatma Gandhi, do not seem to realize that the acts of the people are merely the results of their beliefs inculcated upon their minds by the Shastras and that people will not change their conduct until they cease to believe in the sanctity of the Shastras on which their conduct is founded. No wonder that such efforts have not produced any results. You also seem to be erring in the same way as the reformers working in the cause of removing untouchability.

To agitate for and to organize inter-caste dinners and inter-caste marriages is like forced feeding brought about by artificial means. **Make every man and woman free from the thralldom of the Shastras, cleanse their minds of the pernicious notions founded on the Shastras, and he or she will inter-dine and inter-marry, without your telling him or her to do so.**[9]

Therefore, the dynamics of inter-caste marriages can be succinctly understood from Ambedkar's exposition, for inter-caste marriages become an important means to annihilate caste. Inter-caste marriages break down the divisions of caste and try to affirm the equality of both the spouses. Therefore, it is appropriate to propagate inter-caste marriages among different communities and castes as our response.

Reimagining Christian Public Witness in India

Christian public witness, in the context of the demonic caste system, is both a challenge and a call for us all that are called to be faith communities. It is high time that we cast out the demon of caste system, and that is the one-point agenda in our Christian witness in the context of violence and violation of human rights. Here are some pointers as we reread selected biblical texts, which give us some impetus in moving forward in our faith journey.

Rereading Genesis 4: 1-16: The blood of the innocent cries for justice

Brothers Cain and Abel were divided by their occupation, one as tiller of the land and the other as keeper of the sheep. Human kind, who were supposed to be living as brothers and sisters, had to fall prey to the mischievous device of Manu, who wanted to classify communities based on their occupations, and thus the caste system came into force. We have Cain, who represents a certain caste, and Abel, another caste. When they both brought in their offerings and Abel's offering was well-accepted, and Cain's was not accepted, Cain made a hate campaign against his brother and took him to his field and killed Abel because he could not take his defeat, which was a defeat for his whole community.

Cain today represents the dominant Vanniyar community, who cannot take that their sibling community, the Dalits, have emerged victorious by the very act of inter-caste marriage. It is not that Cain's offering was not accepted, but it was because Abel's offering was accepted that he was killed. The same operating system works here today. Cain probably killed his brother Abel in the field and was trying to project that it was either a suicide or an accidental death. It was not until God asks, "Where is your brother Abel?", that Abel's body was found.

When God asks Cain about Abel, he replies, "I do not know; am I my brother's keeper?" This is the same kind of reply that we see today in the context of Ilavarasan's murder, where the dominant communities reply, "I do not know; am I my brother's keeper?"; the same response comes from several groups.

In verse 10, we see God replying, **"What have you done, listen, your brother's blood is crying out to me from the ground."** The blood of Ilavarasan on the railway track was calling to God and all those faith communities seeking for justice. Ilavarasan, like Abel, could not speak aloud to tell that he was tortured (for Cain rose against him), that he was oppressed because of caste prejudices, that he had been murdered by the casteist forces, and his blood lay there to speak to God.

Christian public witness in such a context, therefore, is:

- To acknowledge that we are our brother's and sister's keepers, trying to be conscious of our contexts, trying to analyse the conflicts in the name of caste. Christian public witness is to be the conscience keepers of our society.

- To give up falsehood, for if we do not speak at the moment of murder and violence, the stains of blood would speak and challenge our communities. In the case of Ilavarasan, his blood became a testimony, challenging caste prejudices and calling the attention of the world to address the evils of caste.

- When several Abels are being slaughtered on the altar of caste, we as faith communities need to be prophetic in speaking justice to the dominant groups.

Rereading Ruth: Inter-tribal marriage as building communities of justice

The story of Ruth and Boaz is a well-known text that speaks of inter-tribal, inter-territorial marriage, to which the lineage of Jesus Christ is traced. Ruth was a Moabite, a landless young widow and had to glean the fields for her livelihood. Boaz was from a rich family of Elimelech and was the owner of the land. Had Boaz refused to marry Ruth, just because she was from a foreign land and from a different culture, trying to be exclusive with his tradition, Ruth would have been left alone all her lifetime. When love sparked between them, no religion, no territory, no caste or creed came in their way; the commitment to the love for one another paved the way for building communities of equality and peace. Boaz's dominant community, rather than opposing their wedding, stood as witness to their union and coming together. From that lineage came Jesse, then David and then Jesus Christ. I guess this was a conscious choice of God to send Jesus Christ through a lineage of inter-tribal marriage, and I am sure Jesus would have been proud of his inter-tribal lineage. A saviour had come from an inter-caste marriage. Ilavarasan and Divya, if they were allowed to live together, would have been an exemplary couple overcoming the prejudices of caste and power.

Therefore, the Christian public witness in such a context is:

- To consciously encourage inter-caste marriages among communities of different faiths.

- To build communities of justice and peace by promoting inter-caste marriages in various places and contexts; and for the church to become a hub of inter-caste, inter-creed unions and special wedding liturgies to be written for such contexts.

Rereading Matthew 20: 1-16: Locating God among those standing still at five o'clock

The parable of the labourers in the vineyard, as found in Matthew 20: 1-16, narrates the story about the landowner who hires workers at 6 in the morning, at 9 in the morning, at noon, at 3 in the afternoon and at 5 in the evening. Those who were strongly built, who were experienced and had a very promising CV, were employed in the very first round of interview. Those who were less qualified but had other strengths were later employed at the next hour, and those who had even fewer qualifications but probably had some other skills like communication were later employed by the employer to work in his vineyard. In verse 6 we see the landowner going to the marketplace even at five in the evening to see some people standing around to seek some work for the day. He then asks them, "Why are you standing here idle all day?" and in verse 7, they reply, "Because no one has hired us."

Why is no one hiring these people? What could have been the reasons for their not being employed? Probably these people standing at 5 p.m. would not have been able to compete in a competitive world around; those with higher class and society define merit and thereby determine the norms for merit, describing them as incapable of work. Probably, these people still standing eagerly to be employed even at 5 p.m. could be people with disabilities and people who are mentally challenged, for no one wants to employ them because of their disabilities; all able-bodied people were preferred and given work in the earlier hours of the day. Probably these people still standing eagerly to be employed even at 5 p.m. could be women, for no one wants to employ them because of their being branded by the patriarchal society with their gendered stereotypes as being incapable of working. Probably these people still standing eagerly to be employed even at 5 p.m. could be transgender persons, for no one wants to employ them because of their sexuality and discriminate against them in all jobs. Probably these people still standing eagerly to be employed even at 5 p.m. could be people from Dalit and Tribal communities, for they do not have the same nurturing as the others have had and are denied chances of employment in many cases.

The writer of the parable in verse 7 even brands these people standing at 5 p.m. as "idle," implying that the rest of them who were employed earlier seem to be smart and meritorious. In such a context, the landowner shifts the locale from that of tradition and exercises justice by not only employing these people who are still standing at 5 p.m. but also by giving equal wages to all, even those who started to work from the first hour, angering those who came early. Economic justice is ensured on the basis of equity and equality.

In our times today, where the mantra of globalisation is profit without any importance to human worth, where forces like patriarchy, caste, class and fundamentalism rule as principalities and powers prefer those with so-called capabilities and employ them at early hours, the parable calls us to shift our locales to those who are still standing at 5 p.m. to be employed and recognised. In the changing landscapes of the church and society, the call for all of us is to shift our focus to those who are standing at 5 p.m., eager to be employed, for no one hires them because of the stigma and discrimination they face. May this, therefore, call upon us all to locate God among those who are still waiting at 5 p.m. and recognise the worth of a life that has been equally granted by God to all. Unless we shift our locale to those friends and communities on the margins and make them the epicentre of our missioning, our faith may not have its savour and relevance. Shall we, therefore, rise up to the occasion of affirming life in all its fullness among those who are being pushed to the margins by the forces of class, caste, gender, and strive to break down these cruel forces, for God stands among those who are still waiting at 5 p.m. to be employed and to receive equal wages like others.

People like Ilavarasan are one among those who are still standing at five in the evening because they come from the Dalit community. When he got married to the so-called community from 3 p.m., there was violence and bloodshed, and eventually he was murdered by the forces of the evil caste system. The call for Christian public witness in such a context is:

- To locate, explore and situate God among those Ilavarasan communities who keep standing till 5 p.m., hoping to be called.

- To recognise and give a preferential option to those at 5 p.m. and bring them into the mainstream to be on an equal footing with the rest of the communities.

- To mission for the cause of those people who have been standing all through the day, hoping against hope for equity and equality.

Conclusion

Ilavarasan's death is indeed a wake-up call for all committed and responsible citizens, irrespective of identities of different religious affirmations, to join hands in fighting the demonic caste system. It was expressed that: "Ilavarasan's tragic death is an indication that progressive forces need to come out more forcefully against the intermeshing of caste and patriarchy.

Whether it is the middle-class families of India of growing cities or the Khap panchayats of rural north India or criminal politicians, it is becoming clear that caste cannot be fought without fighting patriarchy."[10] I wish and hope that this *kairos* moment shall be captured by us all to stand and speak for justice in all our localities to build networks and partnerships among committed people to carry the flame of this moment and get caste and its various forms eliminated from our land.

Allow me to conclude with a personal letter that I have written to Ilavarasan, after his death.

Dear brother Ilavarasan,

I know you are no more with us to receive this letter as I write to you, but I know that you from eternity are listening and looking to us in silence. In the absence and silence from all quarters, it was your innocent blood which drew the attention of God crying for justice, and thereby now calling us all to awake and speak for justice. I write to you confessing our insensitive attitudes towards the evil forces of caste. You, in the context of violence and violation of rights, stand as an epitome and an inspiration for commitment to love and liberation. Your life has testified to the very fact that "love is selflessness and self is lovelessness." Keep talking to us my friend Ilavarasan. As I speak to you, we pledge that we would give up caste practices in our churches, communities and societies. We commit to prevent many other Ilavarasans from being murdered by caste and its cruel manifestations. To us, faith communities, your life has taught us a lesson that 'God is not like Doreamon giving gadgets to the needy Nobitha to overcome the strife, but God works through bold and courageous people like you and many others like you who are committed to become martyrs for the cause of love and liberation.' You live in our hearts, for your love for equality and justice will keep inspiring and influencing many generations of young people now to the ones that are to come in future.

Long live Ilavarasan.

Endnotes

1 http://kafila.org/2013/07/16/ilavarasan-at-a-deadly-new-junction-of-caste-and-electoral-politics/

2 http://www.dnaindia.com/analysis/1857647/editorial-dna-edit-we-failed-ilavarasan

3 "Fighting Caste Fighting Patriarchy" Editorial, *Economic and Political Weekly*, Vol XLVIII No.29, July 20, 2013, 8.

4 Felix Wilfred, *Asian Public Theology: Critical Concerns in Challenging Times,* (New Delhi: ISPCK, 2010), 30-32.

5 http://www.thehindu.com/todays-paper/tp-national/tp-tamilnadu/educated-caste-hindu-youth-campaign-against-intercaste-marriages/article3644332.ece

6 "Fighting Caste Fighting Patriarchy," Editorial, *Economic & Political Weekly*, Vol. XLVIII No.29, July 20, 2013, 8.

7 http://en.wikipedia.org/wiki/Inter_caste_marriage

8 Sanjay Paswan and Paramanshi Jaideva (Eds). *Encyclopedia of Dalits in India. Vol.I*, (Delhi: Kalpaz Publications, 2002), 221.

9 Dr. Babasaheb Ambedkar Writing and Speeches, http://ambedkarquotes.wordpress.com/2007/07/12/inter-caste-marriage-detailed/

10 "Fighting Caste Fighting Patriarchy," Editorial, *Economic & Political Weekly*, Vol. XLVIII No.29, July 20, 2013, 8.

Chapter 9

Fighting Impunity:
The Saga of a Victim of Torture
Reflection on Esther 1

Ground Zero

"Fighting Impunity" has been a campaign in support of victims of torture, and this aptly suits our contexts as the most heinous crimes committed in our land, be it in the name of caste, religion, gender, class or region, are all committed with utmost impunity. The oppressive forces, the perpetrators of violence, take for granted the fragile situations of our times and continue to violate the rights of people; they go free in the end for they have the shield of impunity around them. Impunity is the affirmation of the status quo, the principalities and powers of unjust systems and the failure of the state to investigate the violations and to bring to justice those perpetrators of crimes. In the infamous Tsundur case in Andhra Pradesh, where some 20 Dalits were brutally massacred, the accused were let go on the pretext of insufficient evidence after about two decades of investigation. The same happened after the violence against Dalit

Christians in Kandhamal, Odisha, in 2008. There are scores of such stories, where the victims of violence continue to be victims of torture while the perpetrators enjoy impunity and continue their oppression. The same cry for justice resonates in the recent Badaun case of the rape and killings of Dalit girls in Uttar Pradesh, and in the global context, in the oppression in the name of occupation of the Palestinians. The saga of the victims of torture know no bounds, and their plights are not being heard and justice is a faraway dream for such people.

The Saga

The first chapter in the book of Esther in the Bible has an interesting story of a woman who became a victim of torture at the hands of her husband, who was sufficiently guarded by his royal impunity, and ultimately faded away from the records of the scripture, risking gospel for the sake of gospel. Her saga is a testimony and a challenge for all of us to commit ourselves to be in solidarity with the victims and in pooling support for all the victims of torture today. She is the bold and the beautiful royal Queen Vashti.

Her Excellency Queen Vashti was the royal Queen to King Ahasuerus who ruled from India to Ethiopia with over 127 provinces in his kingdom. The king threw a party for his leaders from all his provinces in order to show his riches of royal glory and splendour. The queen also gave a banquet to the women in the palace. When the party was at its peak and when the heart of the king was merry with wine, he ordered to bring Queen Vashti, dressed in wearing her royal crown, in order to show the people and the princes her beauty. Queen Vashti refused the king's command and consequently became a victim of the king's anger and she lost her crown.

Queen Vashti, the Victim of Indignity

When the king ordered her to do a catwalk on his royal ramp, Queen Vashti denied the king's order, for she strongly believed in self-respect and self-dignity. For the queen, her values were more prominent in life and no force or person could either influence her values or compel her to compromise her values. The queen knew that refusal and disobedience to the king's order would cost her dearly. Despite being conscious of the consequences, she was bold enough to stand for her dignity. By refusing to display her beauty, Queen Vashti displayed her inner beauty of self-dignity. The cost of self-dignity was a dethroning as she became a victim to the forces of indignity and indecency.

Queen Vashti, the Victim of Patriarchy

For King Ahasuerus, his queen, the woman, was yet another material like his riches and wealth. As he showed off the riches of his kingdom to his guests, he thought he could show off the external and physical beauty of his wife, Queen Vashti, and make his guests happy and joyful. The king did not realise that beauty and human sexuality are the gifts of God that need to be respected in all solemnity and sacredness. The forces of patriarchy governed him and, therefore, he could not respect his wife as his equal partner in life. On listening to the other men, he was forced to pass a decree that any woman who does not obey the commands of her husband will have to face similar consequences as the queen. Queen Vashti, so, became of victim of patriarchy.

Queen Vashti, the Victim of Torture

Imagine the plight of Queen Vashti, who was thrown out from her palace to the streets of her kingdom for sticking to her values of self-dignity and self-esteem. She was sent away from her husband's house on to the streets, and the men of her country would have laughed at her and would have mocked and insulted her, even teased her, "Vashti, who wanted to be the mother of self-dignity, who wanted to be the forerunner for women's rights, is now on the streets without any shelter." She became a divorcee, a single woman, and her pain must have known no bounds.

Patriarchal forces try to take advantage of single women, even one who had been a queen, and Queen Vashti would have undergone trauma and torture that was unbearable and unexplainable. Moreover, the king called for fresh applications to the post of his wife—someone who would please him, adding to the torture she was undergoing. There would have been great mental agony and emotional torture for Queen Vashti. In silence and in loneliness, she bore the torture for the sake of her values and principles. There would not have been any space for her to share or ventilate her feelings; all her feelings would have piled up within her. If I may be allowed to stretch my imagination, I would probably think Queen Vashti would have died from the torture from all quarters of life and that is why there is no mention of her again in the scriptures. From royalty to indignity, the torture of Queen Vashti continues to this day in the many lives of women.

Challenge

On 26 June, which we observe as the United Nations International Day in Support of Victims of Torture, Queen Vashti's saga of torture comes afresh. Even today, many Dalits are beaten up, ostracised, humiliated and even killed. The plight of Dalit women is beyond words; everyday Dalit women are raped, abused and murdered. Dalit children are among the worst victims of child labour; most are undernourished and are used and abused in life.

Dalits continue to be the victims of torture today. Violence on Dalits has been a common phenomenon and the discrimination against Dalits over the years has become subtle, yet aggressive. But neither the legislature nor the judiciary has been listening to their pains. Sixty-plus years of waiting for justice, imagine the trauma of victimhood. Torture has become the common denominator with which all Dalits in India live today. Palestinian friends continue to face similar torture and illegal detention by the occupiers and face hardships, with justice and liberation a distant reality.

On a day in support of the victims of torture, and in the light of Queen Vashti's saga of torture, consider this: who really did come in support of the queen? The scripture is absolutely silent on it, and it is likely that none dared to come in support of the dethroned queen. As a victim of torture, Queen Vashti had to stand all alone. Who dared to come in support of her? None of her relatives came in support of her fearing the king's decree; none of her friends came in support of her; none of her prayer partners came in support of her; none of her community members came in support her; none of her temple partners came in support of her; none of the royal wives of the princes in their provinces came in support of her; none of the kingdom authorities like the women welfare ministries came in support of her; none of her co-women in her provinces came in support of her (how sad the kingdom spread from India to Ethiopia, and there was none to be with her and stand for her); no one came in support of her, for everyone feared the wrath of the king. Queen Vashti had to live without support and had to live the torture all through her life; what torture it would have been. Unbearable and unthinkable! On the other hand, the king enjoyed impunity, for no one dared to speak against the king. Queen Vashti fought impunity in her silence and risked being forgotten from scriptural tradition, for she was a fighter standing for her own convictions of self-dignity. She is an epitome of poise and resistance. Where is God in this text? What is scriptural about this text?

There are many Vashtis today in our societies who live a torturous life. Queen Vashti eventually vanished from the scriptures, but I think her life, her witness and her spirit continues to call all of us today to ssupport all victims of torture; those people who are kept in illegal detention, people who are tortured in the name of caste, abused physically and verbally, beaten, intimidated, threatened, false cases imposed on them, money extorted from them. Let us express our solidarity with these victims and resolve today to address these strategies of victimhood with a commitment to justice. Queen Vashti calls for a response of prevention, reduction and elimination of all forms of torture, to fight impunity at all cost, and to strive for a just and transformed society. Come, let us stand in solidarity with and support the victims of torture from this day on, let us enlarge our tents in bringing support to our fellow brothers and sisters who live in abject trauma.

Chapter 10

When a Thirsty Hagar Speaks…
Based on Genesis 21: 8-21

Early in the morning, long before the sunrise, when it was still dark, Abraham, through whom I bore his first descendant, deserted us and sent us away into the desert. All that he gave was some leftover food and a skin of water before leaving us into the dark.

I did not know where to go with my son and started to walk through the wilderness, for that is where I came from. Coming from a Black ethnic minority community, an outcast community, I was treated as a property of my master at their house and was inhumanly pushed out from their house. After a brief walk in the woods, my child felt hungry and I gave him food and water. Towards the end of the day in that scorching sun in the desert, we were thirsty and couldn't continue our walk. We woke up the next day thirsty and searched for an oasis in that desert and could not find any water. I couldn't bear to see my son dying of thirst, and I left him alone near a bush and was sobbing at the other end, for God alone could save us from this thirst. I might be the only woman, perhaps the only slave woman, who had a conversation with God in the scriptures, calling God 'El -Roi' (God who sees). Yet, Abraham, who couldn't overcome his patriarchal dominance, deserted me and my son. And we were dying of thirst.

At that moment, God saw our plight and heard our cries. In fact, the patriarchal writers of the text in Genesis did not record my plight and cries and they mention that God heard the cries of my child. Yes, God did hear the plight of my son, for God gave life by quenching our thirst with a well of water. God sent an angel and strengthened me by providing us water. Water was life to me and my son, for through water my child was ordained to become a great nation.

I realised that without water, life is nearly death. For I have seen it with my own eyes, for my son was nearing death from thirst and was longing for fresh water. By drinking water from the well, Ishmael my son came back to life. When my son and I were dying of thirst, God sent an angel with water from a well. God's response is accurate, timely and relevant. Even though Abraham deserted me and my son, God did not leave us nor forsake us. God gave us the waters of life so that we become a stream of life for many generations.

As I narrate this story, I recount several people across the world in the twenty-first century who are dying of thirst, lacking water, in fact, lackingfresh water. My experience echoes several peoples' experience today. Like me, there are many who are 'quintessentially outsiders,' marginalised through gender, social class, caste and ethnicity, and have been yearning for fresh waters to save their lives.

I see, like me, many Hagars in Dalit communities today, for whom death appears so near through the denial of water.

One of the ways through which the caste people expose their segregation and discrimination of Dalits is by denying access to water, by not allowing them to draw water from the same wells or hand pumps they use. More than 20 per cent of Dalits do not have access to safe drinking water, while only 9.84 per cent Scheduled Caste households have access to sanitation, and most Dalits depend on the mercy of the upper castes to allow them access to water. Dalit women have to walk long distances to fetch water for their families, which has several ramifications in terms of rights and health. Added to this, for Dalits who are dependent on land, the livelihood of the entire family is dependent on the woman, and the inability to access water means denial of right to life. The violation of a basic human right such as water reveals the cruel indignity of the caste system.

The God of Hagar is a God who sees and is a God who hears, for the God of justice sees and hears the cries and tears of communities who have been living under stigma, discrimination and exclusion. The God of Hagar comes to thirsty communities with wells of fresh water, quenching their thirst and granting life. When Hagar speaks, she exposes the powers of patriarchy of the faithful. When Hagar speaks, she invokes a God who sees and hears the plight of thirsty communities, thirsty for justice and peace. When Hagar speaks, she is firm in addressing the thirst of her children. When Hagar speaks, she overcomes stigma and discrimination inflicted by caste and such other prejudices. Let those that have ears listen to Hagar and strive for a just world, where water will be accessed by all people freely and justly.

Questions for Discussion

1. Identify the Hagars in your own community who are nearing death from thirst. Discuss how you can address the issues of thirst in your own context. How can you be a water angel in your community?

2. If you were an additional character in this text, who would you be and how would you quench the thirst of Hagar and her son Ishmael?

3. Analyse the nexus between caste, gender, class, race and thirst? Who are thirsty and why are they pushed into situations of thirstiness?

Chapter 11

To Paul: A Letter from Onesimus
In Response to Philemon 1

Dear father Paul,

Onesimus, a liberated person in Christ Jesus, a freed slave from Philemon.

To Paul, my dear father who showed God's grace to me as a fellow prisoner in Rome—also to Timothy, Epaphras, Mark, Aristarchus, Demas, Luke, to Junia, Lydia, Priscilla, Phoebe, Tabitha, Chloe, and several other women whose names have been forgotten and erased, who support Paul and his fellow workers in Christ—and to the house churches that you keep travelling and writing to:

Grace and peace to you from God our liberator and the Lord Jesus Christ, who has freed us from all bondage.

I always thank our God for your passion for the gospel of Jesus Christ. Specially I thank you for your letter to Philemon appealing him in love to seek reconciliation with me. I know your love for Christ, love for the church and your love for people. I thank you for building partnerships among people, transcending the barriers of class and ethnicity and thereby giving a true meaning to *koinonia.* Your love and discipleship of Christ has given me great joy and encouragement in strengthening our church for love, because you my father and brother have refreshed and inspired the hearts of God's people.

Therefore, I appeal to you on the basis of love as you have appealed to Philemon in my case. It is none other than Onesimus—a man to be judged by the content of the Christian character and not to be judged by the colour of my skin or by the status I previously held as a slave, for I am freed from slavery and bondage by Christ Jesus and I remain to enjoy that liberation Christ has granted me. I appeal to you as a son who shared prison and prison experiences with you, for we both experienced suffering under the Empire and knew what it was to be in chains, although my chains were different from yours. Formerly, when I was a slave, I was considered useless, was treated as property, looked down as subhuman and was subjected to all kinds of humiliation for I was perceived as a nonperson.

As I explained to you the kinds of torture and suffering I and my household have had to endure because of slavery are huge. Those sufferings made me strong as a person to resist them and stand for a just system where all human beings are treated equally. For the cause of promoting life, for the cause of envisioning a just society and for the cause of giving a liberative legacy to my children, I had to run away from Philemon. I was imprisoned for such an act, and that's where the love of Christ encountered me through your fellowship.

I specially want to thank you for taking my debt on you and prove how important a Christian value it is to cancel debts of poor people as an important mark of Christian discipleship. By taking my debt on you, you have shown me in practice the love of Christ who took my debts on him on the cross, for I could experience it in my life. Thank you also for writing to Philemon to receive me as he would receive you, once again emphasising the importance of welcoming and receiving everyone in the love of Christ. In that reception as exhorted by you, my brother Philemon has received me as a brother, as a member of his family. I knew what it was to be a slave in his household once, and I also have experienced his love as a family member, which was because of the love of Christ. Ever since then Philemon has treated me as a partner in the mission of God, and we have continuedS to work together for the realisation of God's kingdom here on earth. Many wondered what a beautiful sight it was to see the master and his previous slave work together as brothers and partners, which was because of the love of and for Christ.

On a final note, dear father Paul, allow me to appeal to you to call any practice of any form of slavery as sinful and unchristian, for in Christ we are all one. Any form of racism, casteism, discrimination, exclusion, oppression, patriarchy, trafficking, child labour and such other practices that are modern forms of slavery do not fit in with the gospel of Jesus Christ, and therefore we as a church should resist such forms and stand in solidarity with those on the margins and strive for justice in every given context. Christ has come to set people like me free and I will work to liberate all people who are chained in any form of bondage as a gospel calling for me.

You are always welcome to come and stay with us and enjoy our indigenous hospitality. My wife and children and all our churches join me in sending their greetings to you.

The grace of our Lord and liberator Jesus Christ, the love of God, who calls us to freedom and dignity for all people, and the communion of the Holy Spirit who partakes in all our struggles for peace be with us all, now and forever.

Your fellow worker in Christ,
Onesimus

Relevance

1. Encourages to listen to and read stories from the margins of our contexts as our faith imperative. *Mission as storytelling, where stories are from the margins.*

2. Establishes a *koinonia* of God's people, transcending all kinds of barriers of race, ethnicity, gender, ideologies, perspectives and theologies. *Mission as building inclusive partnerships.*

3. Celebrates difference with a sense of humility and openness towards others' perspectives and positionings. *Mission as celebrating diversity.*

Can we Reimagine a Public Witness
Interrogating Caste in India and in our Church?

*N. Paul Divakar**

After at least 400 years as a missionary church, here in India, it should not come as a surprise that the church in India is basically a Dalit-Adivasi church. The church in India has consisted mostly of Dalits and Adivasis since the early times. Raj Bharat Patta has brought this out beautifully throughout in all the chapters. It is also clear in the history of the early missionaries in the southern part of India. But has the church stood in defence of the rights of Dalits and Adivasis? While in its theological interpretations there is no doubt of this fact that Christ Jesus has come to liberate the oppressed and break their chains, in practice the institution of the church has swung away from this understanding. There is a need to bring accountability of the church and its powers and institutions to the theology of the oppressed.

In the late nineteenth century, clashes within the church clashes within the church existed over this very question. The clashes between the Syro-Malankara rites and the Latin rite within the Catholic Church have caste at its base. The Syro Malankara rite tried to protect the purity of the Church while it closed its doors to Dalits and the fisherfolk. This created the Latin rite separate for the fisherfolk and some Dalits. A similar tension existed between the Syrian Christian Church, which is of the dominant castes, and Pratyashka Raksha Daiva Sabha (PRDS) and its founder Poikayil Yohannan, a Dalit leader who differed and resisted casteism within the Syrian Christian church and started PRDS as liberation of Dalits both within the church as well as in society.

Even prior to this, in the seventeenth century, there were opposing views of proselytisation in the Catholic Church in western and southern India. One group was led by Goncalo Fernandez and the other by Roberto de Nobili among the Society of Jesuits of the Catholic Church. Roberto de Nobili believed that caste and caste practices of purity and pollution in society can be tolerated as long as the dominant castes accepted Christianity. Roberto de Nobili further insisted that he should move away from the 'Pirangi' Christians, the coverts from among the fisherfolk and Dalits and locate himself in the Brahmin agrahara (the locality of Brahmin 'highland') in order to steer the church away, stigmatised as it was as the church of the outcastes. Here for Roberto de Nobili, the crux of Christianity was not about equality of human beings but about the people of nobility accepting Christ as their lord.

The context that we are in and the debate we are having is not new. This has been plaguing the church in India since the early Orthodox period, from AD 54 through the Portuguese missionary church in the early seventeenth century to that of the CMS missionary church in the early nineteenth century. This conflict continues today in the twenty-first century, with, on the one hand, Dalit Christians demanding the same protection given to non-Christian and non-Muslim Dalits and on the other Archbishop Antony Pappusamy of Madurai Archdiocease of the Catholic Church denying any allegation of discrimination against Dalits, which is the official view of the Government of India; that is therefore denying any protection that is constitutionally the right of Dalits.

There are three critical questions Bharat has raised which we as church and as members of the body of church need to ask ourselves.

Why is it that we are unable to agree on the anathema of the practice of casteist values within the Christian faith?
We need to talk about caste in today's church. We need to debate the issue. Why are we as church leaders and members of congregations completely avoiding a debate or discussion on the implications of being caste-driven? What is it that we are afraid of? Are we afraid that caste will consume us, will overpower the church? Are we afraid that the only informal identity we take refuge in, 'the caste' or 'our caste', will no longer be available to us now? Do we think that a life without the boundary or the privileges or restrictions that caste place on us will vanish and make us vulnerable to being 'equal' or 'on a par' with all 'others'? Are we afraid as is being observed in the Syrian Orthodox Church or the strategy of de Nobili that real Christianity is among the dominant castes or is possible only with the participation of the dominant castes? Will not the church have any recognition of value without their participation?

Why cannot we accept Dalit Christians' multiple layers of identity as long as the law itself discriminates Dalits on the basis of faith or religion.

The duality or triality of the identity—the deep dilemmas and the crisis of identity this crates, the pain and the torment and the guilt this creates—is unexplained and then there is value judgement that many priests and pastors inflict upon the church members.

The struggle of Dalit Christians through the multiple identity tactic has to be seen as a symbol of resilience. We are in an 'exile mode' of practice of our faith. We are not yet ready for the liberative mode. For Dalit Christians these multiple identities serve as a symbol of resilience in overcoming their experiences of pollution and marginality that they have been undergoing. The marginality of Dalit Christians pushed many Dalit Christians to martyrdom in Kandhamal in Odisha.

Can we proclaim the good news to the excluded?

The Bible clearly says that we need to stand up for the rights of Dalits and Adivasis and other marginalised communities who are being lynched, massacred, tortured, murdered, raped, killed and whose property is destroyed. Can the church be a sanctuary for those who are facing these crimes? How can we extend support as a church and as its members?

Can the church define *Dalitekklesia* as a reimagined public witness in India; can the church speak out against caste atrocities and speak up for the victims of violence of caste and patriarchy?

We need to stand up not just for the right of representation or reservation for Dalit Christians but also for Dalit right to land, rights against exploitation, Dalit women's rights and the right to clean environment. It needs to have gender justice at its core, upholding the rights of children and also of the LGBTQI. This needs to be kept at the centre of *Dalitekklesia.*

In other words, can we wipe away the sin of casteism? The sin of untouchability in all its forms? We need to stand as a witness against any form of these practices in our families, and in our churches when casteism raises its head in any form. We are also called to stand up against these even in secular bodies we work.

We are clear that as Christians and as a church, we cannot serve both Christ and caste.

The National Council of Churches in India (NCCI) took a strong stand way back in 2010 proclaiming for the first time that 'No one can serve Christ and Caste' and initiated a campaign 'Solidarity with Dalits for Justice and Dignity.' Theologically, it is crystal clear that the tenets of casteism are totally opposed to the meaning of salvation. Bharat has brought these out very clearly through the perspective of the most marginalised in our society and urges us to reimagine our public witness through *Dalit Missiology* which we have most neglected in our church bodies as well as in our own families. It is now our responsibility to put these into action in our lives and our congregations and in our ministry of whatever field we may be in.

***Adv. N. Paul Divakar** is the Convener of the Global Forum on Discrimination Based on Work and Descent. He also serves as the Chairperson of the Asia Dalit Rights Forum (ADRF). He is one of the founding members of the National Campaign on Dalit Human Rights (NCDHR). He was voted by *Outlook* magazine as one of the 50 most influential Dalit leaders in India.

www.ingramcontent.com/pod-product-compliance
Lightning Source LLC
Chambersburg PA
CBHW061445150726
47987CB00001B/336